WORDS

FROM THE

WHITE HOUSE

LEXICAL BOOKS BY PAUL DICKSON

The Congress Dictionary: The Ways and Meanings of Capitol Hill
(with Paul Clancy)

The Dickson Baseball Dictionary
(second and third editions, *The New Dickson Baseball Dictionary*)

A Dictionary of the Space Age

Drunk: The Definitive Drinker's Dictionary
(updated as *Intoxerated*)

*The Hidden Language of Baseball: How Signs and Sign-Stealing
Have Influenced the Course of Our National Pastime*

Journalese: A Dictionary for Deciphering the News
(with Robert Skole)

*Labels for Locals: What to Call People from
Abilene to Zimbabwe*

*Names: A Collector's Compendium of Rare and Unusual,
Bold and Beautiful, Odd and Whimsical Names*

Slang: The Topical Dictionary of Americanisms

*War Slang: American Fighting Words and Phrases
Since the Civil War*

*Words: A Connoisseur's Collection of Old and New, Weird
and Wonderful, Useful and Outlandish Words*

WORDS

FROM THE

WHITE HOUSE

WORDS AND PHRASES
COINED OR POPULARIZED BY
AMERICA'S PRESIDENTS

PAUL DICKSON

WALKER & COMPANY

NEW YORK

Published by Walker Publishing Company, Inc., New York
A Division of Bloomsbury Publishing

All papers used by Walker & Company are natural, recyclable products made from wood grown in well-managed forests. The manufacturing processes conform to the environmental regulations of the country of origin.

LIBRARY OF CONGRESS CATALOGING-IN-PUBLICATION DATA
HAS BEEN APPLIED FOR.

ISBN: 978-0-8027-4380-0

Visit Walker & Company's website at www.walkerbooks.com

First U.S. edition 2013

3   5   7   9   10   8   6   4   2

Book design by Gretchen Achilles

Printed and bound in the U.S.A. by Thomson-Shore, Inc., Dexter, Michigan

Necessity obliges us to neologize.

—THOMAS JEFFERSON

CONTENTS

CHARTING THE PRESIDENTS AND THEIR NONLEXICAL FIRSTS

As a means of introducing the presidents in their proper order, here they are listed along with some of their firsts, many of which involve the means of communication, from the birth of the post office to today's social media. The idea being to show the context into which they amended and enriched the language.

1. **GEORGE WASHINGTON**, 1789–1797—First president.

2. **JOHN ADAMS**, 1797–1801—First to live in the White House.

3. **THOMAS JEFFERSON**, 1801–1809—First to wear long trousers.

4. **JAMES MADISON**, 1809–1817—First to have had prior service as a congressman; first to have an inaugural ball.

5. **JAMES MONROE**, 1817–1825—First to be wounded in battle; Rutherford B. Hayes would be the second.

6. **JOHN QUINCY ADAMS**, 1825–1829—The first president to be photographed, but the photo was not taken while he

was in office; the first and only president to have a son whose given name was George Washington.

7. **ANDREW JACKSON**, 1829–1837—First to travel by train. On June 6, 1833, he traveled from Ellicotts Mills, Maryland, to Baltimore by the B&O Railroad. He was the first president born in a log cabin—a mark of humble distinction. (Chester A. Arthur was the last born in a log cabin.)

8. **MARTIN VAN BUREN**, 1837–1841—First president born in the United States. All previous presidents were born before the United States became a country, although all were born in places that would later be parts of the United States.

9. **WILLIAM HENRY HARRISON**, 1841—First president to die in office. He served for a single month.

10. **JOHN TYLER**, 1841–1845—First to become president upon the death of another. He was also the president with the most children: fourteen.

11. **JAMES KNOX POLK**, 1845–1849—First president to have his inauguration reported by telegraph.

12. **ZACHARY TAYLOR**, 1849–1850—First president to win office in an election that was held on the same day (November 7, 1848) in every state.

13. **MILLARD FILLMORE**, 1850–1853—First president to have a stepmother.

14. **FRANKLIN PIERCE**, 1853–1857—The first president born in the nineteenth century (1804). Pierce installed the first central-heating system in the White House. He is the only president to have said "I promise" instead of "I swear" at his inauguration.

15. JAMES BUCHANAN, 1857–1861—First and only president who never married.

16. ABRAHAM LINCOLN, 1861–1865—First Republican president; first president with a beard and the first born outside the original thirteen colonies.

17. ANDREW JOHNSON, 1865–1869—First to be impeached (acquitted by a single vote).

18. ULYSSES SIMPSON GRANT, 1869–1877—First president to view the Pacific Ocean (1852).

19. RUTHERFORD BIRCHARD HAYES, 1877–1881—First president to graduate from law school; first White House telephone was installed, by Alexander Graham Bell himself, during the Hayes administration. First Easter egg roll on the White House lawn was conducted by Hayes and his wife.

20. JAMES ABRAM GARFIELD, 1881—First left-handed president; first president to campaign in two languages—English and German.

21. CHESTER ALAN ARTHUR, 1881–1885—First president to take oath of office in his own home and the first president to have been accused (wrongly) of not being born in the United States.

22. GROVER CLEVELAND, 1885–1889—First president to appear in a film. In 1895, Alexander Black came to Washington and asked Cleveland to appear in his photoplay *A Capital Courtship*. He agreed to be filmed while signing a bill into law.

23. **BENJAMIN HARRISON**, 1889–1893—First president to have a Christmas tree in the White House.

24. **GROVER CLEVELAND**, 1893–1897—First and only president to serve two nonconsecutive terms.

25. **WILLIAM MCKINLEY**, 1897–1901—First to ride in an automobile.

26. **THEODORE ROOSEVELT**, 1901–1909—First president to entertain an African-American guest at the White House—Booker T. Washington. First president to win the Nobel Peace Prize.

27. **WILLIAM HOWARD TAFT**, 1909–1913—First president of the Union of forty-eight states.

28. **WOODROW WILSON**, 1913–1921—First president to earn a Ph.D.

29. **WARREN GAMALIEL HARDING**, 1921–1923—First president to speak on the radio, as well as the first to have broad newsreel coverage, which means it can be argued that he was our first media president; first to own a radio and first to ride to his inauguration in an automobile.

30. **CALVIN COOLIDGE**, 1923–1929—The first inaugural address broadcast by radio was that of Coolidge, on March 4, 1925. He was also the first born on the Fourth of July—July 4, 1876. (Three presidents died on July 4th: John Adams and Thomas Jefferson on July 4, 1826, and James Madison on July 4, 1831.)

31. **HERBERT CLARK HOOVER**, 1929–1933—First president born west of the Mississippi, the first engineer, first (and

only) to speak fluent Mandarin Chinese, and first to have an asteroid named for him.

32. **FRANKLIN DELANO ROOSEVELT**, 1933–1945—First president to fly in an airplane during his term of office and later the first to have a presidential plane. The first to appear on television, when he opened the New York World's Fair in 1939. The first president to visit South America while in office. He was the first president to appoint a woman, Frances Perkins, as a cabinet member (secretary of labor). First president whose mother was eligible to vote for him. His was also the longest administration—twelve years, one month, and eight days.

33. **HARRY S TRUMAN**, 1945–1953—First president to travel underwater in a modern submarine; the first to give a speech on television.

34. **DWIGHT DAVID EISENHOWER**, 1953–1961—First president to appear on color television; the first to be president of all fifty states.

35. **JOHN FITZGERALD KENNEDY**, 1961–1963—First Roman Catholic president.

36. **LYNDON BAINES JOHNSON**, 1963–1969—First to take the oath on a plane and the first sworn in by a woman. He did both in 1963 after President John F. Kennedy died. First to use a teleprompter.

37. **RICHARD MILHOUS NIXON**, 1969–1974—First to visit all fifty states, first to speak with a human on the moon, first president to resign from office.

38. **GERALD RUDOLPH FORD**, 1974–1977—First and only president not to be elected to the presidency, or the vice presidency; first president to pardon a former president; first to visit Japan; first to have been an Eagle Scout.

39. **JAMES EARL CARTER JR.**, 1977–1981—First president born in a hospital—the Wise Clinic in Plains, Georgia, on October 1, 1924.

40. **RONALD WILSON REAGAN**, 1981–1989—First divorced president and the first to wear contact lenses. At sixty-nine, Reagan was the oldest elected president. Dying at ninety-three years of age, Reagan lived longer than any other president.

41. **GEORGE HERBERT WALKER BUSH**, 1989–1993. First president born in June (presidents have now been born in every month of the year); first president to have flown in combat; first and only president to publicly refuse to eat broccoli.

42. **WILLIAM JEFFERSON CLINTON**, 1993–2001—First to have been a Rhodes scholar. His second inauguration (1997) was the first broadcast live online. People worldwide tuned in on the World Wide Web. First to have an e-mail address.

43. **GEORGE WALKER BUSH**, 2001–2009. First president to hold an MBA; his 2002 State of the Union was the first to be live broadcast on the Internet

44. **BARACK HUSSEIN OBAMA**, 2009–. First to use Facebook and Twitter and have a YouTube account. First African-American president and first born outside the contiguous United States (Hawaii).

INTRODUCTION

BRAVE NEW WORDS

I n 1608, one year after the establishment of Jamestown, Captain John Smith attempted to transcribe the Algon-quian word meaning "he scratches with his hands" by writing down *rahougcum*. This led to the word *raccoon*, and one of the earliest seeds for American English was sown. Smith's arrival in Virginia coincided roughly with Shakespeare's writing of *Timon of Athens* and *Pericles*.

More than three centuries later, in 1951, Mitford M. Mathews of the University of Chicago Press published the two-volume work *A Dictionary of Americanisms on Historical Principles*, which contained fifty thousand American words and phrases along with their definitions and extensive notations on their origins. These included words adopted from native tongues, such as *skunk, squash, pawpaw,* and *raccoon,* as well as words from other languages—*cafeteria* from Spanish, *sleigh* and *coleslaw* from the Dutch. Other words were concocted from what Mathews called "the old lumber" of British English: *bullfrog, rocking chair,* and *catfish,* as well as thousands of words and phrases straight out of the American experience, from which we learned to play ball, eat crow, bark up the wrong tree, and paddle one's own canoe.

When one browses through this work and the earlier *Dictionary of American English*, which Mathews worked on with the British lexicographer Sir William Craigie, one is taken with the number of words and phrases that were coined, first recorded, or made popular by the nation's presidents, beginning with George Washington.

Indeed, the largest number of White House words have been handed down from the *founding fathers*—a term created by Warren G. Harding for his "front porch campaign" of 1920. Thomas Jefferson alone gets credit for more than one hundred new words—among those that survive are *lengthily*, *belittle*, *electioneering*, *indecipherable*, *monotonously*, *ottoman* (the footstool, not the empire), *pedicure*, the noun *bid*, and, appropriately, the verb *neologize*.

The early presidents felt that creating new words and new uses for old ones was part of their role in creating an American culture. "I am a friend to neology," Thomas Jefferson wrote to John Adams in 1820. "It is the only way to give to a language copiousness and euphony." And the early presidents had Noah Webster and his followers at hand to legitimize their brave new words.

Jefferson and others of his time felt that Americans were more tolerant of innovation in speech and writing than those in England and thought that American innovations might eventually justify calling the language of America by a name other than English.[1]

There was also a sense that a new descriptive American language needed to be created that was distinct from the prescriptive King's English. This new American English and other cultural phenomena (free libraries, public schools, and copyright protection) were, as Noah

NOAH WEBSTER

Webster termed them in a letter to Benjamin Franklin, "acts of defiance." Webster himself coined the term *American-English* in his first dictionary (1806) when he predicted, "In fifty years from this time, the American-English will be spoken by more people, than all the other dialects of the language."

Many on both sides of the Atlantic were alarmed that Americans were adding words to "their" language. As Mitford M. Mathews pointed out in a later work called *American Words*, "They thought the English language belonged to those who lived in Great Britain and that Americans should show their appreciation of being allowed to use it by not making any changes to it."[2]

Webster considered this notion foolish and plunged into the task of creating a dictionary of the American language. He announced on the Fourth of July, 1800, "New circumstances, new modes of life, new ideas of various kinds, give rise to new words and have already made many material differences between the language of England and America." This statement was offensive to the defenders of the status quo, including one of Webster's former tutors at Yale University, who wrote, "Let then the projected volume of *foul and unclean* things bear his own Christian name and be called NOAH'S ARK!"

British critics savaged the concept of American English. Samuel Taylor Coleridge asserted in 1822 that "the Americans presented the extraordinary anomaly of a *people without a language*. That they had mistaken the English language for baggage (which is called *plunder* in America), and had stolen it."[3]

Undaunted, Webster went about collecting words of the early leaders of not only the Republic and its institutions but also those of the indigenous people—*creek* for example as an alternative to *brook*—and the nascent frontier.

When the first edition of Noah Webster's dictionary appeared in 1806, one critic was outraged when he came upon two words that had never appeared before in a dictionary: *presidential* and *congressional*. These words were denounced as "barbarous," and he said that they were "unnecessary, and offensive to the ear."

Some—if not most—of these early presidential terms were not pure coinages but words that a president was the first to leave in a written record. Others were created by aides and associates and passed along to the president. Yet even this is fascinating—how, for example, did it come to be that the first written record of the onomatopoetic word *bobolink* was by John Adams, or that nobody before James Madison had used the word *squatter* to mean someone occupying property or territory that was not his or her own?

Many of the words attributed to George Washington appear in his diaries as simple terms that Allan Metcalf in his book *Presidential Voices: Speaking Styles from George Washington to George W. Bush* describes as "connected with home and farm" and were probably in general use around Mount Vernon and other Potomac plantations. The thirty-seven terms Washington is given credit for in the *Oxford English Dictionary (OED)* include *cradlers* (farmhands who reap with a cradle scythe, 1766),* *logged* (describing a house made from logs, 1784), and New Town Pippin (a special a variety of dessert apple with a yellowish-green skin and aromatic flesh, 1760).

Over the years, a number of words have been attributed to presidents that later were found to have been used by others in print before they did, or the word was used in a different sense. The sources of these attributions were earlier editions of the *OED* and were based on assumptions made by researchers working before the luxury of electronically searchable proprietary databases such as ProQuest Historical Newspapers. These revised attributions are updated as they are discovered and appear in the subscription-based online edition of the *OED.* Two examples: *ravine* (George Washington) and *public relations* (Thomas Jefferson). But by the same token, these search engines are putting other words in the mouths of other presidents.

But the fact remains that the early years of the Republic were a crucible for American leaders as neologists. John Adams, to cite another example, brought us a number of new words, including *caucus.* John Quincy Adams brought us *gag rule.*

The tradition of American presidents coining new words and phrases continued throughout the rest of the nineteenth

---

*A frame of wood. A tool for reaping grain with fingers attached to the snath (also snathe or snaithe)—the handle—to catch the cut grain by means of a row of long curved teeth projecting above and parallel to a scythe, for laying grain in bunches as it is cut.

century as many innovations took the form of campaign slogans. Election slogans, badges, buttons, and sometimes elaborate paraphernalia were indigenous to the new nation. Certain words and phrases seem to show up only at election time when candidates go on *the hustings* to give *stump speeches*, while working the *rubber-chicken circuit* trying to *stay ahead of the curve* while rallying *grassroots* support.

American politics took on the cant and slang of the frontier and the poker table, and the people of the rest of the world were at once stunned and amused as they noted that only in America were there *bandwagons* to jump on, *coattails* to attach to, and *war chests* to dip into.

There were also pure coinages. Abraham Lincoln, for example, came up with *relocate, relocation*, and the great metaphor for the Civil War: *a house divided*.

The tradition blossomed again at the turn of the twentieth century with a steady parade of new coinages, beginning with Theodore Roosevelt's *lunatic fringe, mollycoddle*, and, appropriately, *bully pulpit*, as well as some wonderful TR phrases and aphorisms such as *Speak softly and carry a big stick.* "Theodore Roosevelt struck off like sparks from a horseshoer's anvil word combinations that have burned their way into our everyday speech," wrote a columnist in 1947.

Roosevelt, who boasted that "no president ever enjoyed himself in the presidency as much as I did," seemed to have a recreational fascination with new ways of expressing himself.

The trend continued throughout the twentieth and into the twenty-first century, but no coinages were more dominant than the link between governing and the card table. There were square deals, new deals, and fair deals, and President Truman had a sign on his desk that said THE BUCK STOPS HERE.

THE PURISTS AND THE PRESIDENTS

By the nature of the microscope under which they are observed, presidents are more likely than the rest of us to have words or phrases attributed to them that they did not coin. Presidents are also more likely to come under fire for "impurity" of speech or for their disregard of the "rules" of English—or, even worse, for using words that are undignified.

During the July following his inauguration, Abraham Lincoln sent a message to Congress opposing secession threatened by Southerners. The message said in part, "With rebellion thus sugar-coated they have been drugging the public mind of their section for more than thirty years, until at length they have brought many good men to a willingness to take up arms against the government." The Hon. John D. Defrees, the government printer, was disturbed by the use of *sugar-coated*. He finally went to Lincoln, with whom he was on good terms, and told him that a message to Congress was a different affair from a speech at a mass meeting in Illinois—that the message became a part of history and should be written with that in mind.

"What's the matter now?" Lincoln inquired of the printer.

"Why," said Defrees," you have used an undignified expression in the message." He read the sentence aloud and suggested Lincoln replace the word.

"Defrees," replied Lincoln, "that word expresses precisely

my idea and I am not going to change it. The time will never come in this country when the people won't know exactly what 'sugar-coated' means."[4]

As if to raise the hackles of the purists, in 1904 Theodore Roosevelt wrote to Thomas R. Lounsbury, a professor of English at Yale University, to say that he approved of splitting infinitives. Warren G. Harding came under constant attack in many quarters for his use of *normalcy* and *bloviate* and was singled out by H. L. Mencken for his use of the "one-he" combination (as in "one does as he wishes"), but Harding was vindicated when a group of twenty-nine philologians took a vote on "one-he" and twenty-two found it acceptable English.

Woodrow Wilson may have been the first president taken to task for his use of slang. He was cited for using such phrases as "we must get a move on" and "that is going some." Wilson also was criticized for pronouncing *ordinary* as "ornery" and for omitting the definitive—and honorific—article before the word *Congress*. The Congress had been the norm for several generations until Wilson came along. The next three presidents restored the article, but it eventually drifted away save for formal papers and documents. Wilson also raised eyebrows with neologistic aphorisms such as, "A man's rootage is more important than his leafage."[5]

PAUL DICKSON

Franklin D. Roosevelt's lexical critics looked down their noses on his willingness to use street slang (*chiseler* for swindler) and for creations such as *iffy*. President Eisenhower was castigated for his reliance on words that were common in the military. When he used *finalize* in his second State of the Union message, it set off a clamor among the grammatical purists, aka the language police. As the lexicographer Bergen Evans observed a few weeks later, "Columnists, editorial writers, and teachers pounced on the unlucky word, labeling it 'nonexistent,' 'hideous,' 'atrocious,' and 'meaningless.'"

Finalize had been in use in government and business circles for years, but the clamor underscored the point that every word uttered by a president is subject to extraordinary scrutiny. Evans, a grammarian of the first order, noted that the word Ike had dared to utter served a useful purpose beyond such words as *finish*, *complete*, or *conclude*.[6]

Gradually, Americans allowed presidents more freedom in their use of slang. In 1985, President Ronald Reagan, discussing presummit maneuvering, told a group of wire-service reporters that the time had come to "stop this 'futzing' around."*

Yet there was less forgiveness when it came to errors and slips of the tongue. Perhaps no president has been so strongly criticized for his linguistic miscues as George W. Bush. The linguist Mark Liberman of the Language Log website has suggested that Bush was not unusually error-prone in his speech: "You can make any public figure sound like a boob, if you record everything he says and set hundreds of hostile observers to combing the transcripts for disfluencies, malapropisms,

---

*futz = Slang based on Yiddish *arumfartzn*, to fart around.

word formation errors and examples of non-standard pronunciation or usage . . . Which of us could stand up to a similar level of linguistic scrutiny?"[7]

"The best course is to let the purists howl," wrote Bergen Evans. "They have been grousing throughout our history while about them the language has prospered—often with an assist from the President."

INS VS. OUTS

The following A–Z presidential lexicon features not only the coinages, redefinitions, and adoptions of the presidents themselves but also words, phrases, and slogans created for them by aides and advisers. Words created or popularized by first ladies and vice presidents are included, as are occasional words from other leaders. Several words from British prime ministers—notably Winston Churchill and Benjamin Disraeli—are included because they have had an influence on the American presidency, as well as words used to describe presidents: e.g., Representative Patricia Schroeder's *Teflon president* for Ronald Reagan, and presidential eponyms—all of which seem to belong in a book like this and reflect the overall charm of presidential speech.

I.

HAIL TO THE WHITE HOUSE: WORDS, PHRASES, AND SLOGANS— A TO Z

ADMINISTRATION. The term during which a president holds office. **George Washington** from his Farewell Address: "In reviewing the incidents of my administration, I am unconscious of intentional error."

ALICE BLUE. A pale greenish-blue created by a dress designer in homage to **Theodore Roosevelt**'s daughter Alice, born in 1884; later she became Alice Roosevelt Longworth. Attesting to the popularity of the color was the song "Alice Blue Gown," recorded by various artists including Frank Sinatra. In his *Browser's Dictionary*, John Ciardi points out that the Roosevelts are the

only family to have given the language two eponyms—*Alice blue* and *teddy bear*.[1]

AMERICA FIRST. Cast as a slogan by **Woodrow Wilson**: "Our whole duty, for the present [1915, during World War I] is summed up in this motto, 'America First.' The motto suggests we should think of America before we think of Europe in order that America may be fit to be Europe's friend."[2] In his 1920 campaign, **Warren G. Harding** put a new twist on Wilson's America First: "It's an inspiration to patriotic devotion to safeguard America first, to stabilize America first, to prosper America first, to think of America first, to exalt America first."

AMERICANISM. Allegiance to the traditions, institutions, and national ideals of the United States. The word *Americanism* was coined by **John Witherspoon** (1723–1794), president of the College of New Jersey (now Princeton University) and signer of the Declaration of Independence, in reference to words or phrases distinct from British use. Witherspoon wrote in 1781 that the word described "phrases or terms, or a construction of sentences, even among persons of rank and education, different from the use of the same terms or phrases, or the construction of similar sentences in Great-Britain. The word Americanism, which I have coined for the purpose, is exactly similar in its formation and signification to the word Scotticism." **Thomas Jefferson** gave the word a secondary meaning in the sense of an attachment to the United States and its values in a letter to fellow signer of the Declaration Edward Rutledge on June 24, 1797, in which he wrote of "the dictates of reason and pure Americanism." **Warren G. Harding** won a landslide victory in 1920 by promising a return to traditional American ideals—"normalcy" and adherence to "Americanism." He later admitted, "I don't know much about Americanism, but it's a damn good word with which to carry an election." **Theodore Roosevelt** was more definitive: "Americanism means the virtues of courage, honor, justice, truth, sincerity, and hardihood—the virtues that made America. The things that will destroy America are prosperity-at-any-price, peace-at-any-price, safety-first instead of duty-first, the love of soft living and the get-rich-quick theory of life."[3]

AMERICANIZE. To make American in form, style, or character. The word was coined by **John Jay**, **George Washington**'s secretary for foreign affairs. In 1787 he wrote to John Trumbull, "I wish to see our people more Americanized, if I may use that expression; until we feel and act as an independent nation, we shall always suffer from foreign intrigue."[4] (John Trumbull, who would later become Jay's secretary, was a respected artist whose painting *Declaration of Independence* was used on the reverse of the $2 bill. A commemorative 6¢ postage stamp shows him with sword in hand at the Battle of Bunker Hill.)

ANALYZATION. The action or process of analyzing; analysis. This word was used by **George W. Bush** on June 23, 2000: "This case has had full analyzation and has been looked at a lot. I understand the emotionality of death penalty cases." It was thereafter cited as a Bushism, another mangled coinage from the chief executive. A quick consult of the *Oxford English Dictionary* shows that this is a respectable word, dating back to 1698.[5]

ANGLOMAN. An admirer or partisan of England. A creation of **Thomas Jefferson** first recorded in 1787 in a letter to John Adams: "It will be of great consequence to France and England to have America governed by a Galloman or Angloman." (A galloman, by the way, is a francophile.) Jefferson had a low regard for this person whom he had named. He wrote in a letter to James Madison, "I never doubted the chicanery of the Angloman."[6]

ANGLOMANE. **John Adams's** adoption of the French word for a person exhibiting the symptoms of Anglomania, which he used to describe a partisan or advocate of English (or British) interests in North America: "The parties of rich and poor, of gentlemen and simplemen, unbalanced by some third power, will always look out for foreign aid, and never be at a loss for names, pretexts and distinctions. Whig and Tory, Constitutionalist and Republican, Anglomane and Francomane, Athenian and Spartan, will serve the purpose as well as the Guelph and Ghibilline." [7]

ANGLOMANIA. An excessive fondness for that which is English. This term of derogation was coined by **Thomas Jefferson** in 1787 in a letter to Madame de Corny, a formidable hostess in Paris at that time: "I know your taste for the works of art gives you a little disposition to Anglomania."[8] Jefferson also created a synonym for *anglomania*: *anglomany*, which he used as the opposite of *Americanism*.

ANGLOPHOBIA. Fear or dread of England (or Britain), its people, culture, etc., created by **Thomas Jefferson**. In May

1793, a French frigate had arrived at Philadelphia with a captured British ship. Jefferson wrote to James Madison: "We are going on here in the same spirit still. The Anglophobia has seized violently on three members of our council."[9]

ARSENAL OF DEMOCRACY. It was during his December 29, 1940, radio fireside chat that **Franklin D. Roosevelt** coined the phrase to describe America's  industrial heartland, which was already gearing up for worldwide conflict. Barely two months after the December 7, 1941, attack on Pearl Harbor, the last civilian automobile rolled off a Detroit assembly line as the auto industry made a stunningly quick conversion to produce everything from tanks and trucks to bombers and ammunition.

AS MAINE GOES . . . SO GOES THE NATION. This maxim of presidential elections dates back to 1840 when it began as a campaign slogan of **William Henry Harrison**, a Whig who defeated the incumbent Martin Van Buren. As John Ciardi explained in his last book on the mother tongue, *Good Words to You*, "At that time because of the wintry blasts of November, Maine's election was held in September. Its returns were in, therefore, about six weeks before the rest of the election of the country, and Harrison supporters could not resist making a slogan of their clear victory." As the Whigs became Republicans and began to dominate the state, they continued to use the slogan—now as a portent of victory—even after Election Day in Maine was moved to the same day as in the rest of the nation.

Less true now than in its original coinage, it nevertheless has many offspring. "As the baby boom generation goes, so goes the nation," wrote George F. Will in *The New Season: A Spectator's Guide to the 1988 Election.* Or, recalling George McGovern's trouncing as the 1972 Democratic nominee, Everett Carll Ladd Jr. in *Where Have All the Voters Gone?* offered, "As goes Massachusetts, so goes the District of Columbia."

AUTHENTICATION. The action or process of authenticating, or proving the accuracy or legitimacy. Credit to **Thomas Jefferson** in 1788: "So numerous are the writings presented, that their authentication alone, would occupy the greater part of his ["the Minister Plenipotentiary for the United States of America" to France, i.e., Jefferson himself] time."[10]

AVERAGE. To form a mean or medium sum or quantity. The word appears in Noah Webster's 1828 dictionary and had its written debut in **George Washington**'s Diary: "Killed a Wether . . . being a middlesized one . . . The above [Washington's estimates of its gross and dressed weight, tallow, wool, skin, and the monetary worth of each] appears to be no more than the worth of a fat Wether—it being imagind, that they woud average the above weight and 3d. pr. lb. [Washington's estimate of the going rate for the meat of his wether] is a low price at this Season of the year [February]."[11] (A wether is a male sheep, a ram.)

AXIS OF EVIL. Coined by speechwriter David Frum for **George W. Bush** in his 2002 State of the Union address. Bush used it to describe governments he accused of helping encourage terrorism and weapons of mass destruction. In his autobiography, *Decision Points*, Bush wrote, "In my State of the Union address, I had outlined the threats posed by Iraq, Iran, and North Korea. States like these, and their terrorist allies, constitute an axis

of evil, arming to threaten the peace of the world. The media seized on the phrase 'axis of evil.' They took the line to mean that the three countries had formed an alliance. That missed the point. The axis I referred to was the link between the governments that pursued WMD and the terrorists who could use those weapons. There was a larger point in the speech that no one could miss: I was serious about dealing with Iraq."[12]

BABY RUTH. The name of a log-shaped candy bar made of caramel and peanuts, covered with chocolate, that many have long assumed was named after the baseball player Babe Ruth. The Curtiss Candy Co. introduced the candy bar in 1921 and priced it at 5¢; it soon became one of the hottest-selling candy bars on the market. The company's "official" explanation was that the bar was named after "Baby" Ruth Cleveland, the first-born daughter of former president **Grover Cleveland**, despite the fact that Ruth had died of diphtheria at age twelve in 1904. The notion that a candy bar called Baby Ruth should appear on the market at a time when Babe Ruth, the slugger, suddenly became the most famous ballplayer in America is seen as a noticeable coincidence. Robert Hendrickson sheds additional light on the situation: "When another company got Babe Ruth to endorse Babe Ruth's Home Run Candy in 1926, Baby Ruth's manufacturer appealed to the Patent Office on the grounds of infringement and won, the Babe's candy bar never appearing." The candy bar is now manufactured by Nestlé. The

Irish dramatist George Bernard Shaw, becoming exposed to baseball, is said to have asked an American journalist, "Who is this Baby Ruth? And what does she do?"[13]

"THE BACKBONE OF A CHOCOLATE ÉCLAIR." As undersecretary of the navy, **Theodore Roosevelt** attempted to undermine his boss, William McKinley by declaring this to be part of his makeup.

BAILOUT. Hardly a new word or idea, bailout was key to the Obama economic plan and was looked up so often at Merriam-Webster's website that the dictionary publisher made it the 2008 Word of the Year. At number 2 was *vet*—as in to vet a running mate. "There's something about the national psyche right now that is looking up words that seem to suggest fear and anxiety," said John Morse, Merriam-Webster's president and publisher. Other top words, based on volume of lookups: *trepidation, precipice, turmoil, maverick,* and *bipartisan.*

BAKING. That which bakes; that which is hot enough to bake. "The ground, by the heavy rains . . . and baking Winds since, had got immensely hard," is how **George Washington** first used this adjective in 1786.[14]

"BEFORE THIS DECADE IS OUT." Rallying cry for a moon landing in **John F. Kennedy**'s special message to a joint session of Congress on urgent national needs, May 25, 1961. "First, I believe that this nation should commit itself to achieving the goal, before this decade is out, of landing a man on the moon and returning him safely to the earth . . . I believe we should go to the moon. But . . . there is no sense in agreeing or desiring that the United States take an affirmative position in outer space, unless we are prepared to do the work and bear the burdens to make it successful."[15]

BELITTLE. To make small; to reduce in size. **Thomas Jefferson** coined the word in his 1788 *Notes on the State of Virginia.* In criticizing a French naturalist who had written negatively about the natural wonders of the New World, he wrote, "So far the Count de Buffon has carried this new theory of the tendency of nature to belittle her productions on this side of the Atlantic."

H. L. Mencken later asserted in *The American Language* that the word set off "a storm of abuse" by critics on either side of the Atlantic. It was immediately condemned in the *European Magazine, and London Review.* "*Belittle!*" wrote the reviewer. "What an expression! . . . For shame, Mr. Jefferson! . . . O spare us, we beseech you, our *mother-tongue!*"

Noah Webster liked this word and put it in his 1828 English-language dictionary, but in a new edition published twenty years after his death, the word included the note: "[*Rare* in America. *Not used* in England.]"

In 1872, the American scholar Fitzedward Hall decided the time had come to kill *belittle*, which kept showing up in his reading: "It has no visible chance of becoming English; and as the more critical writers of America, like all those of Great Britain, feel no need of it, the sooner it is abandoned to the incurably vulgar, the better."* The professor's crusade failed, and the word—along with its offspring *belittler* and *belittling*—is used everywhere the language is spoken, although as late as 1937, H. W. Fowler declared in his *Modern English Usage* that "it is still felt by many to be an undesirable alien."[16]

BID. The offer of a price, the amount offered, specifically at an auction. The first evidence of this word as a noun according to the *Oxford English Dictionary* occurs in a letter from **Thomas Jefferson** to James Madison in 1788: "Littlepage who was here as a secret agent for the King of Poland rather overreached himself. He wanted more money. The King furnished it more than once. Still he wanted more, and thought to obtain a high bid by saying he was called for in America and asking leave to go there."[17]

BIG TENT. A term that came into play during the first year of the presidency of **George H. W. Bush** in 1989. It was popularized by the Republican political consultant Lee Atwater, who called for the Republican Party to accommodate a broader range of opinion. "Our party is a big tent," Atwater told reporters on November 14, 1989. "We can house many views on many issues. Abortion is no exception." The term had been

---

*Hall also used his book *Recent Exemplifications of False Philology* to attack the use of *bug* for insect, *demean* for disgrace, *parties* for people, and *plenty* for plentiful. Hall became the model for the insufferable critic of new words and was disdainful of any writers who strayed from his idea of linguistic purity. By his standards, Washington Irving and William Makepeace Thackeray were "bad writers." Irving was a neologist in his own right, having coined several terms with staying power, including *the almighty dollar*, which appears first in his story "The Creole Village": "The almighty dollar, that great object of universal devotion throughout our land, seems to have no genuine devotees in these peculiar villages."

used earlier in politics by both Republicans and Democrats, but Atwater put it up in lights.*

BLOVIATE. To speak bombastically or grandiosely and at length. Etymologically, it combines the word *blow*—think *blowhard*—with the *-iate* suffix for a pseudo-Latinate effect. As the former *Baltimore Sun* copy editor and language blogger John E. McIntyre wrote recently, "The word is frequently identified with President **Warren G. Harding**, who, although he did not coin it, used it frequently and whose speeches exemplified its meaning." Harding defined the term in his own manner: "To loaf about and enjoy oneself, to prattle on." This term was in folk speech before Harding, but Harding made it part of the American vocabulary.

The word is in fact much older. In William Safire's *New Political Dictionary*, the word columnist for the *New York Times* traced the word back to 1850 and said it meant "to orate pompously." The *OED* dates it back farther, to 1845: "Peter P. Low, Esq., will with open throat . . . bloviate about the farmers being taxed upon the full value of their farms, while bankers are released from taxation."

---

*In 1975, for example, Democratic House Speaker Thomas "Tip" O'Neill told a reporter, "The Democratic Party is a big tent. We are widely diversified." During the 1980 presidential campaign, the Republican national chairman, Bill Brock, urged the party to embrace a "big tent" strategy. That year, Ronald Reagan won in a landslide over President Jimmy Carter and Republicans gained control of the Senate—the first time they had controlled either house of Congress since 1954.

The word has legs and surfaces from time to time in a new political context. In his *New York Times* column of June 6, 1999, Frank Rich announced that he had made up a new word—*bloviator*—to describe any TV talking head who at the time was involved in endless speculation about the fallout of Bill Clinton's relationship with Monica Lewinsky. Perhaps because of Rich's column, the 2000 edition of *The World Almanac and Book of Facts* listed *bloviate* (not *bloviator*) as a new word for the year. Bill O'Reilly takes a refreshing attitude in his advice to viewers sending him e-mail: "No bloviating. That's my job."

As Allan Metcalf points out in *Presidential Voices*, "There's something likeable about *bloviate*, just as there was about Harding. He loved to bloviate and was unashamed to use that word for it. What's not to like? As Rabbi Robert J. Marx recently wrote, 'It's more fun to say *bloviate* than to say 'orate verbosely.'"[18]

BLUE SMOKE AND MIRRORS. Verbal sleight-of-hand used to sell a program to Congress or a candidate to the public. The independent presidential candidate John Anderson quipped that **Ronald Reagan**'s economic policies—aka Reaganomics—would need "blue smoke and mirrors" to work. The journalists Jack Germond and Jules Witcover used the phrase as the title for their book on the 1980 presidential election.

BOBOLINK. An American blackbird known for its song, which the *Dictionary of American English on Historical Principles* described as a metallic clinking noise. The bobolink has more than a dozen names, of which some are onomatopoetic of its call. The most dignified name is Robert of Lincoln. The

Oxford English Dictionary, which lists these call-based names under the entry for *bobolink*, cites **John Adams**, before he was elected president, as the earliest written source of the word. In 1774, Adams made the following entry in his diary: "Young Ned Rutledge is a perfect Bob o' Lincoln—a Swallow—a Sparrow—a Peacock—excessively vain, excessively weak, and excessively variable and unsteady—jejune, inane, and puerile." The bobolink may have been commonly known by this name before 1774. Edward Rutledge, who was from South Carolina, was the youngest signer of the Declaration of Independence.

BOMFOG. Acronym for Brotherhood Of Man, Fatherhood Of God. Term that journalists of a generation ago attached to the pious, homily-ridden blather of politicians. It is often referred to as *bomfoggery*. Garry Wills traced the origin of the term in a column in the *Washington Star*. He said it dates back to when **Nelson Rockefeller** was on the presidential campaign trail: "When Nelson was winding up a campaign speech, he liked to orchestrate the coda around 'the Brotherhood of Man under the Fatherhood of God,' and that phrase was a signal to accompanying journalists to sidle back toward the campaign bus."

BOONDOGGLE. A word that has come to mean work or activity that is wasteful or pointless but gives the appearance of having value. The word was not coined by **Franklin D. Roosevelt** but it was made famous by him on January 18, 1936, when he made some informal extemporaneous remarks to the New Jersey State Emergency Council in reference to the programs of the New Deal. "There is a grand word that is going around, 'boondoggle.' It is a pretty good word. If we can 'boon-doggle' ourselves out of this depression, that word is going to be enshrined in the hearts of the American people for many years to come."

There are many posited etymologies for this word, but the most appealing one holds that *boondoggle* was the fanciful invention of Robert H. Link, a Rochester, New York, scoutmaster. He supposedly began using it around 1925 to refer to the ornamental plaited neck cords made by Boy Scouts under his direction, an activity he considered "make-work."

BOOZE. In the campaign of 1840, the Whigs portrayed **William Henry Harrison** as a folk hero and man of the people, and chose the theme and slogan, "Log Cabin and Hard Cider Democracy." Log cabins or facsimiles thereof turned up everywhere. There were log cabin floats decorated with coonskins and log cabin façades on campaign headquarters, and "log cabin cider" freely flowed at campaign rallies. One of the most popular items was a miniature log cabin filled with Old Cabin Whiskey bottled by the E. C. Booz Distillery. Several sources later reported that by the end of the campaign, the word *booze* "had entered the language."

This is almost perfect folk etymology, with some elements that may have contributed to the popularity of an existing slang word for liquor. In fact, the earliest reference to *booze* meaning "alcoholic drink" in English appeared around the fourteenth century, though it was originally spelled *bouse*. The spelling as it is today didn't appear until around the seventeenth century. But this may in fact be a collaborative etymology in which an existing term is given added popularity through a new explanation.

A similar case is the word *hooker* for prostitute, which had been around since at least the 1840s but is popularly ascribed to the disreputable morals of the Army of the Potomac under the tenure of General "Fighting Joe" Hooker beginning in early 1863.

BORK. To block the confirmation of a Supreme Court nominee. This eponymous verb refers to Robert Bork, who was nominated to the Supreme Court in 1987 by Republican president **Ronald Reagan** but was rejected by the Senate by a vote of 58–42, after critics attacked Bork's narrow and conservative interpretations of constitutional protections. In 1991, on the eve of the Senate confirmation hearings for Clarence Thomas's nomination to the Supreme Court, the term was very much in use. "We're going to Bork him," was a widely quoted line about Judge Thomas from Flo Kennedy, a feminist lawyer. *Bork* also can mean to reject any political nominee, as in the Republican admonition not to "bork" John Bolton when his nomination as United Nations ambassador came up for Senate confirmation.

BRAIN TRUST. A group of intellectuals and planners who act as advisers, especially to a government. The term is particularly associated with the presidency of **Franklin D. Roosevelt**. Although the term had been used before with limited success, it was given new life by James Kieran, the president of Hunter College, who used it to describe the group of professors who advised Roosevelt during his 1932 election campaign. It was soon applied to all the new president's close intellectual advisers, who included the professor of government and law Raymond Moley, the law professor and diplomat Adolph Berle, the economist Rexford Tugwell, and the social-welfare organizer Harry Hopkins (whose programs introduced the terms *wider privileged, social worker, welfare, welfare worker,* and *welfare recipient* to millions of Americans). The brain trust during the early days of the Roosevelt administration met nightly to devise and plan New Deal legislation in an undisclosed location known only as "a little red house in Georgetown."[19]

BREADSTUFF. Cereal, flour, meal, etc., out of which bread is made; also bread of all kinds. The word was created by **Thomas Jefferson** in 1793 when he wrote that "France received favorably America's breadstuff." John Pickering suggested in *A Vocabulary; Or, Collection of Words and Phrases Which Have Been Supposed to Be Peculiar to the United States of America* (1816) that this word made headway in America because we lacked the general word *corn,* having used that word exclusively for maize.

BRONC. A slang synonym for bronco, an untamed horse. **Theodore Roosevelt** either coined it or was the first to write it down, in his book *The Wilderness Hunter: An Account of the Big Game of the United States and Its Chase with Horse, Hound, and Rifle*: "I saddled up the bronc' and lit out for home."[20]

BRINKSMANSHIP. A policy that allows the country to risk all-out war in order to get the enemy to back down. The word got its impetus from President **Dwight D. Eisenhower's** White House, probably coined by Secretary of State John Foster Dulles, who had no doubts about the concept. "The ability to get to the verge without getting into the war is the necessary art," Dulles said in an interview early in 1956. "If you cannot master it, you inevitably get into war. If you try to run away from it, if you are scared to go to the brink, you are lost."

The word *brinksmanship* came from **Adlai Stevenson** and the Democrats in the 1956 presidential campaign, who charged Eisenhower and Dulles with brinksmanship.[21]

"THE BUCK STOPS HERE." Harry Truman's adopted phrase for "the responsibility rests here," i.e., the buck cannot be passed any farther. A sign THE BUCK STOPS HERE, which was on Truman's desk in his White House office, was made in the federal reformatory at El Reno, Oklahoma. Fred M. Canfil, then United States marshal for the Western District of Missouri and a friend of Mr. Truman, saw a similar sign while visiting the reformatory and asked the warden if a sign like it could be made for President Truman. The sign was made and mailed to the president on October 2, 1945. Approximately 2½ inches high and 13 inches long and mounted on walnut base, the

painted glass sign has the words "I'm From Missouri" on the reverse side. It appeared at different times on his desk until late in his administration.

The saying "the buck stops here" derives from the slang expression "pass the buck," which means passing the responsibility on to someone else. The latter expression is said to have originated with the game of poker, in which a marker or counter, frequently in frontier days a knife with a buckhorn handle, was given to the person whose turn it was to deal. If the player did not wish to deal, he could pass the "buck," as the counter came to be called, to the next player.[22]

On more than one occasion, President Truman referred to the desk sign in public statements. For example, in an address at the National War College on December 19, 1952, Mr. Truman said, "You know, it's easy for the Monday morning quarterback to say what the coach should have done, after the game is over. But when the decision is up before you—and here on my desk I have a motto which says 'The Buck Stops Here'—the decision has to be made." In his farewell address to the American people in January 1953, Truman referred specifically to this concept: "The President—whoever he is—has to decide. He can't pass the buck to anybody. No one else can do the deciding for him. That's his job."

BULL MOOSE. Name for a short-lived political party that ran in 1912 with former president **Theodore Roosevelt** as its candidate. It had begun as the Progressive Party but was renamed by Roosevelt on October 14, 1912, in Milwaukee moments after he had been shot by a deranged saloon owner. "Friends," he began, "I shall ask you to be as quiet as possible. I don't know whether you fully understand that I have just been shot; but it takes more than that to kill a Bull Moose. But fortunately I had my manuscript, so you see I was going to make a long speech, and there is a bullet—there is where the bullet went through—and it probably saved me from it going into my heart. The bullet is in me now, so that I cannot make a very long speech, but I will try my best."[23]

TR's Bull Moose third party split the Republican voters during the election and enabled Woodrow Wilson, the Democratic candidate, to be elected president. Wilson, a progressive, became one of the few "minority" presidents—he did not get a majority of the popular vote. Wilson got 41.9 percent and Taft got only 23.2 percent. But Wilson scored big in the Electoral College, with 435 votes to TR's 88 and Taft's 8.*

At the time of his death in January 1919, Roosevelt still carried in his body the bullet from the assassination attempt.

BULLY PULPIT. The authority of the president to advocate for a particular agenda or idea, not by legislation but by persuasion. The ability to use the "bully pulpit" is based purely on the president's moral authority and the public's respect for the office of the presidency. The term was coined by **Theodore Roosevelt**, who used the word *bully* as an adjective meaning "superb" or "wonderful," with no relationship to the noun *bully*, i.e., a harasser or someone who preys on the weak.

The term *bully pulpit* comes down to us in an interesting context. It first appeared in print in 1909, embedded in an editorial in the *New York Times* that was highly critical of the Roosevelt administration. The editorial was published on the final morning of Roosevelt's presidency, only hours before the inauguration of William Howard Taft. Although the *Times*

---

*The previous minority presidents were John Quincy Adams, Rutherford B. Hayes, and Benjamin Harrison. And since then, of course, George W. Bush in 2000.

editorial saw good in Roosevelt, it disapproved of his excesses. It noted, among other things, that Roosevelt was "careless with his weapons, and the missiles he has sped somewhat at random in the general direction of rich malefactors have too often found lodgment in the bosoms of the indigent righteous, whose yells have swelled the anti-Roosevelt chorus, while their gore still reddens the field." The bully pulpit was mentioned in the context of what the newspaper called "his immense egotism" and his intoxication with his power to speak and act. The example used came from Lyman Abbott, the American Congregationalist theologian, editor, and author, who was with Roosevelt when he read to a few friends a presidential message. When he finished reading, he wheeled about and said, "I suppose my critics will call that preaching, but I have got such a bully pulpit!"

Although buried in a quote in a very long editorial—it took up a full five of the seven columns of the editorial page—the term was repeated in a letter to the *Times* the next day and several more references were made to it in the weeks following, but only in the *Times* and not in other sources that might seem logical—the *Washington Post, Baltimore Sun, Chicago Tribune*, etc.

Roosevelt used the word *bully* in many contexts but most commonly to report that he was having a "bully time" in the White House, out west, or in Africa. A 1909 editorial the *Springfield Daily Republican* titled "Bully" said, "It is impossible for the foremost citizen of Oyster Bay to escape from the thralldom of the word 'bully'?"[24]

CAUCUS. A private meeting of the members of a political party or political interest group. Either coined or popularized by **John Adams**. The first recorded use of the word is from 1763 in Adams's diary: "This day learned that the Caucus Clubb meets at certain times in the Garret of Tom Daws, the adjutant of the Boston Regiment . . . There they smoke tobacco till you cannot see from one end of the garret to the other . . . They choose a Moderator, who puts Questions to the Vote regularly, and Selectmen, Assessors, Collectors, Wardens, Fire Wards, and Representatives are Regularly chosen before they are chosen

in the Town . . . They send Committees to wait on the Merchants Clubb and to propose, and join, in the Choice of Men and Measures."

There is also evidence that the word had its origin in a native tribal language. Captain John Smith reported in his 1624 *Gener-*

al Historie of Virginia: "In all these places is a severall [separate] commander, which they [the Indians] call Werowance, except the Chickahamanians, who are governed by the Priests and their Assistants, or their Elders called *Caw-cawwassoughes*."[25]

CHEERLEADER. One who leads the cheering at a football game or other sporting or special event. The *Oxford English Dictionary* cites none other than a young **Franklin D. Roosevelt** as presenting the first evidence of the word being used, in 1903: "I was one of the three cheer leaders in the Brown game."

"A CHICKEN IN EVERY POT." Attributed to **Herbert Hoover** in his 1928 presidential campaign—but it was a false attribution. Hoover's Democratic opponent, Al Smith, got hold of a newspaper ad for Hoover headlined A CHICKEN FOR EVERY POT, which had been coined by the Republican National Committee in Washington. Smith used the line to lambaste Hoover. Smith argued that the average workingman could not afford a chicken dinner every Sunday. Hoover cried foul. He did, however, use the phrases "the full dinner pail" and "a full garage." As for the chicken, it came home to roost as part of Hoover's legacy.[26]

The first to use the expression "a chicken in every pot" as a symbol of national prosperity was Henry IV, king of France and Navarre, who said that he would not be satisfied until every family in France could have a chicken in the pot at least once a week. One of his nicknames was "Le Roi de Poule-au-Pot."

"Who But Hoover?" was Hoover's actual prime slogan in 1928, along with "Help Hoover Help Business" and "Hoover And Happiness Or Smith And Soup Houses"; Al Smith campaigned on the less memorable motto "All for Al." Hoover won by promising prosperity under his Republican administration. Unfortunately, the Great Depression kept most pots and garages empty, resulting in an electoral blowout for Franklin Roosevelt four years later. Hoover's slogans in 1932 included "Bring Back Prosperity With A Repub-

lican Vote," "Don't Swap Horses—Stand By Hoover," "Hold On To Hoover," The Worst Is Past," and "It Might Have Been Worse."

CHILD WELFARE. A term encouraged by the first White House Conference on Children in 1909, which was held under the auspices of **Theodore Roosevelt** and, according to Mary Helen Dohan in *Our Own Words*, brought the term "into the vocabulary to join welfare center, welfare administrator, and like combinations, welfare being used for the first time in its modern sense at Dayton, Ohio in 1904." The full name of the Roosevelt conference was the White House Conference on the Care of Dependent Children, and the theme of the gathering was opposition to the institutionalization of dependent and neglected children. According to the *Oxford English Dictionary*, H. G. Wells is credited with the first use of the term in his 1908 work *New Worlds for Old*: "There is the need and opportunity of organizing . . . child welfare."[27]

CIRCUMAMBULATOR. Someone who circles by foot. A creation of Thomas Jefferson, who wrote in 1787, "He [the American explorer and adventurer John Ledyard] was determined to obtain the palm of being the first circumambulator of the earth."[28]

COMPASSIONATE CONSERVATISM. "Compassionate conservatism is neither soft nor fuzzy. It is clear and compelling," George H. W. Bush wrote. "Compassionate conservatism applies conservative, free-market principles to the real job of helping real people, all people, including the poor and disadvantaged." This concept fit with his characterization of a "kinder and gentler nation" because he saw the American dream as too aggressive and unforgiving in its daily pursuits.

COOL. Nice, good. In his *New York Times* column of September 21, 2008, William Safire announced that the earliest use he could find of *cool* in an ironic context—meaning "really something"—is in the political speech Abraham Lincoln gave on February 27, 1860. Safire wrote, "The visitor from Illinois took on those who were threatening secession if an anti-slavery Republican were elected: 'In that supposed event, you say, you will destroy the Union; and then, you say, the great crime of having destroyed it will be upon us! That is cool. A highwayman holds a pistol to my ear and mutters through his teeth, "Stand and deliver, or I shall kill you, and then you will be a murderer!"'"

Before that day was over, Jan Freeman, then language columnist for the *Boston Globe*, issued a dissent in her blog: "Lincoln's 'That is cool' means something more specific than 'that's really something'; today he might say 'What chutzpah!' His highwayman analogy, in fact, is very like the classic example of chutzpah, the guy who kills his parents and then pleads for mercy on the grounds that he's an orphan."

Freeman added, "But this sense of *cool* was not Lincoln's invention, nor even unusual. The 1852 edition of Noah Webster's dictionary has it: '3. Not hasty; deliberate; as, a *cool* falsehood or deception. Hence, 4. Impudent in a high degree, as when speaking of some trick, pretension, &c., we say "that is *cool*.""[29]

COUNTERPRODUCTIVE. Having the opposite of the desired effect. The *Oxford English Dictionary* credits the first use of the word to **Dwight Eisenhower** who on October 3, 1959, at a press conference said: "The holding of a summit meeting . . . would be . . . absolutely impractical and as the State Department says counter-productive." It is doubtful that Ike created this word, but it is true that he brought to his presidency a different vocabulary from his predecessors.

CREEP. Pronunciation imposed from the outside for CREP, the acronym for **Richard Nixon**'s 1972 Committee to Re-elect the President. The variant was popularized before the election—and well before the committee's Watergate-related activities were revealed to the world. Credit for it belongs not to a Democrat, as one might be forgiven for suspecting, but to Senator Robert Dole, chairman of the Republican National Committee. He disliked the way the young know-it-alls on the reelection committee were ignoring the established party apparatus.

CROWDED HOUR. Theodore Roosevelt's "crowded hour" described his attack on Spanish forces at San Juan Hill in Cuba, a compressed time of reckoning, a headlong assault where he proved his skill and bravery on a treacherous battlefield. The term has since been generalized to refer to any moment when one is tested, and it was given new life when Senator John McCain used it to describe his time as a public figure.[30]

CZAR. This title for the omnipotent ruler of Russia in the days before the 1917 Revolution was first used to describe any despotic politician or industrialist and later found its way into other walks of life. The first use of *czar* in the sense the word is used in modern Washington came in 1893 when it was applied to Congressman Thomas B. Reed (R-ME), who insisted on rigid interpretation of parliamentary rules. When Judge Kenesaw Mountain Landis became Commissioner of Baseball in the wake of the 1919 Black Sox scandal—eight members of the Chicago White Sox intentionally lost games—he was given extraordinary powers. Landis was fond of saying, "Czar is what they call me in their papers when they do not call me rogue." Bernard Baruch, appointed by Woodrow Wilson to head the War Industries Board in 1918, was the first to be called a czar. The use of the word, only one year after the Russian Revolution, was originally derogatory, although it is less so today.

Czar was used more frequently in reference to appointed executive branch officials under President Franklin D. Roosevelt during World War II. In 1942, the *Washington Post* reported on the "executive orders creating new czars to control various aspects of our wartime economy."

The word lay fallow for some time until President **Richard Nixon**, who called William Simon, his energy adviser, his energy czar—a nickname, not a job title. Then there came a succession of czars, including a drug czar.

By the time of the Obama administration, when traditional czars had neither a clearly identified mission nor access to the president, they were given a new name by Lurita Doan of Federal News Radio in a November 6, 2009, broadcast: "They are small fish, with little power or impact. In fact, with so few resources allocated, one wonders why the position exists. Just call these guys the czardines—the tiniest political fish—almost certain to be eaten in the big, DC pond."

TR used the term but in a different context: He called some of the minor European monarchs "bush league czars."

DARK HORSE. Politician not known to be a candidate who, at a deadlocked convention, unexpectedly receives the nomination. This term derives from racing slang for a little-known horse that unexpectedly goes to the front. The term made the jump from horse racing to politics in the nineteenth century, when it was applied to a candidate nominated without advance publicity. In *A Browser's Dictionary*, John Ciardi notes that the term was coined by the British statesman and novelist **Benjamin Disraeli** in his book *The Young Duke* (1831): "a dark horse which had never been heard of" swept to triumph. Ciardi reports that the term moved from British track usage to American tracks and then to politics.

"A DAY WHICH WILL LIVE IN INFAMY." A reference to the December 7, 1941, attack on Pearl Harbor, coined by **Franklin D. Roosevelt** when he asked Congress for a declaration of war against Japan. He said, "Yesterday, December 7, 1941—a date which will live in infamy—the United States of America was suddenly and deliberately attacked by naval and air forces of the Empire of Japan." He went on, "The attack yesterday on the Hawaiian Islands has caused severe damage to American naval and military forces. I regret to tell you that very many American lives have been lost. In addition American ships have been reported torpedoed on the high seas between San Francisco and Honolulu." This day of infamy was global. As FDR pointed out later in the speech:

> Yesterday the Japanese Government also launched an attack against Malaya.
>
> Last night Japanese forces attacked Hong Kong.
>
> Last night Japanese forces attacked Guam.
>
> Last night Japanese forces attacked the Philippine Islands.
>
> Last night Japanese forces attacked Wake Island.
>
> And this morning the Japanese attacked Midway Island.

In 1946, an article in the *New York Times* by Cabell Phillips suggested that the phrase was not Roosevelt's but had been created by the speechwriter Raymond Moley or by Robert E. Sherwood, the author and playwright who worked for Roosevelt at the time. Sherwood responded in a letter to the *Times* that "nobody suggested the phrase . . . It was entirely his own." In his *Political Dictionary*, William Safire notes that Roosevelt's first draft of the speech used the phrase "a date which will live in world history," but he substituted "infamy" in the second draft.[31]

DEBARRASS. An ephemeral 1789 coinage of **Thomas Jefferson** meaning to disencumber from anything that embarrasses; to relieve. In a letter from Paris to James Madison on August 28, 1789 (only six weeks after the storming of the Bastille): "Mr. Neckar [*sic* Jacques Necker, director general of France until he was fired by Louis XVI] was yesterday to give in a memoir [memorandum] to the Assembly on this subject [France was broke]. I think they will give him leave to put into execution any plan he pleases, so as to debarrass themselves of this & take up that of the constitution [Declaration of the Rights of Man and of the Citizen]."[32]

DECIDER. A **George W. Bush** coinage for the person who makes the final call, despite consideration of any dissenting voices. In 2006, when the cry to oust Secretary of Defense Donald Rumsfeld had reached a deafening pitch, Bush told the press he himself was "the decider."

DIGITAL DIVIDE. Those who have Internet access vs. those who do not. Vice President **Al Gore's** remarks at the 1998 Digital Divide Event described the Clinton administration's initiatives to bridge the divide.

DOLLAR DIPLOMACY. Promoting the interests of the United States by investment abroad. The term was coined when **William Howard Taft** commented that U.S. operations in Latin America went from "warlike and political" to "peaceful and economic" after the infusion of American money.

DOMINO PRINCIPLE / DOMINO THEORY. Theory named and articulated by President **Dwight Eisenhower** at a news conference on April 7, 1954. Referring to communism in Southeast Asia, he warned of the "falling domino" principle. If one country fell to communism, he said, other countries would begin to fall as well. "You have a row of dominos set up, you knock over the first one, and what will happen to the last one is certainly that it will go over very quickly. So you could have a beginning of a disintegration that would have the most profound influences." Ike's metaphoric use in geopolitics soon grew to the name for the notion that a political event or development in one nation will lead to its occurrence in others.

DO-NOTHING CONGRESS. **Harry Truman** coined the phrase in 1948 in his presidential reelection campaign. As the incumbent, Truman called Congress into a special session that summer to work on legislation ranging from civil rights to an increase in the minimum wage.

"DON'T SWAP HORSES IN THE MIDDLE OF THE STREAM." In 1864, **Abraham Lincoln** ran for reelection as the Civil War raged, and he adopted this as his slogan.* Horses were a much more important element in American life in Lincoln's time than they were in 1936 when **Franklin D. Roosevelt** first ran for reelection, urging voters, "Don't change horses in midstream."

---

*This slogan was used by George W. Bush as well, with detractors parodying it as "Don't change horsemen in mid-apocalypse."

EMBETTER. To make better (antonym to *embitter*). In the words of **George W. Bush**: "I want to thank the . . . people who made the firm and solemn commitment to work hard to embetter themselves." (Bush was also fond of *embetterment*, the state of being emotionally better.) The word was not a George W. Bush neologism; according to the *Oxford English Dictionary*, the word and the meaning date back to 1583.[33]

ENEMIES LIST. Prominent opponents of President **Richard Nixon.** The existence of this list was disclosed by John W. Dean in testimony to the Senate Watergate Committee on June 26, 1973. Responding to a question by Senator Lowell Weicker, of Connecticut, Dean said, "There was also maintained what was called an enemies list, which was rather extensive and continually being updated."

Nixon had personally requested the list from Dean on September 15, 1972: "I want the most comprehensive notes on all of those that have tried to do us in. Because they didn't have to do it . . . If they had had a very close election everybody on the other side I would understand this game. But now [they] are doing this quite deliberately and they are asking for it and they are going to get it . . . We have not used the power in this first four years, as you know. We have never used it. We haven't used the Bureau [the FBI] and we haven't used the Justice Department, but things are going to change now . . . And they're going to get it right. It's got to be done."[34]

By the time Dean testified before the Senate committee, the enemies list included twenty-one organizations and two hundred–plus individuals, among them all twelve African-American House members, some fifty members of the media, assorted business executives, celebrities like Bill Cosby and Barbra Streisand, antiwar protesters, and so on.

"In some circles," wrote Hugh Rawson in "The Words of Watergate," "the list became a badge of honor."*

ENTANGLING ALLIANCES. "Peace, commerce, and honest friendship, with all nations—entangling alliances with none." **Thomas Jefferson** stated this in his inaugural address on March 4, 1801, in reference to U.S. foreign policy, especially in dealing with Europe. This thought had been similarly expressed earlier in a letter to fellow Virginian Edward Carrington, December 21, 1787: "I know too that it is a maxim with us, and I think it a wise one, not to entangle ourselves with the affairs of Europe."

According to research conducted by the Library of Con-

---

*Having a number of acquaintances who were on the list, I can attest to the fact that such a listing was a once and future honor. Just the mention of the list to Daniel Schorr was enough to elicit a broad, proud grin, and Mary Frances Veeck, widow of the baseball maverick Bill Veeck, told me that one of her husband's greatest regrets was not making the list.

gress and contained in *Respectfully Quoted*, George Washington did not use any form of *entangle* but shared a like political view in a letter to Patrick Henry, October 9, 1795: "My ardent desire is . . . to keep the U States free from *political* connexions with *every* other Country. To see that they *may be* independent of *all*, and under the influence of *none*," and to Gouverneur Morris, called the "Penman of the Constitution" for having written the Preamble, December 22, 1795: "My policy has been . . . to be upon friendly terms with, but independent of, all the nations of the earth. To share in the broils of none."[35]

EPA. Initialism for Environmental Protection Agency, U.S. federal agency proposed by President **Richard Nixon** and created in December 1970.

EXPLETIVE DELETED. Term used to replace certain words and phrases in the transcripts of **Richard Nixon**'s presidential tapes ordered by the Watergate Committee. It is not known whether the term was created by Nixon himself or by his secretary, Rose Mary Woods, who was charged with transcribing the tapes with instructions to "take out the rough stuff." At the height of the Watergate crisis that ended Richard Nixon's presidency, transcripts of those once-secret tapes of White House conversations were made public, and the phrase entered the language—often as curse unto itself.[36] *

---

*How vile were the deleted words? As R. W. Apple Jr. wrote in his introduction to the *New York Times* edition of the White House transcripts of the Watergate tapes, "s-h-i-t was the mildest of the deleted expletives."

FAIR DEAL. Policy introduced by **Harry Truman** in his 1949 State of the Union address. According to Truman's special counsel, Clark Clifford, the president wrote in his own handwriting, "Every citizen of this country is entitled to a Fair Deal from his Government." The Fair Deal program had five goals: (1) the attainment of basic human rights; (2) conservation of human resources; (3) conservation of natural resources; (4) expansion of the economy; and (5) attainment of world peace. His Republican opponents called it "eye wash."[37]

Fair deal was a term with an easy link to poker, and Truman was an avid player of the game and a man whom J. R. Dillard, in *American Talk*, termed a "great practical folklorist."

"FATHER, I CANNOT TELL A LIE. I DID IT WITH MY LITTLE HATCHET." Schoolchildren are taught the virtue of honesty via **George Washington**'s famous admission, which enabled him to escape punishment for cutting down his father's cherry tree. The admission and the story are bogus, part of a tale created by Parson Mason Locke Weems in the fifth edition of his *Life of*

George Washington, published in 1806. Weems took the story from the novel *The Minstrel* by Dr. James Beattie, published in 1799 in London.[38]

FAVORITE SON. According to A *Dictionary of American English*, this was originally a commendatory title given to **George Washington** in 1888 as the motto "Freedom's favorite son." It later became a term for a man who has endeared himself to a particular country or state.

FIFTY-FOUR FORTY OR FIGHT. A slogan of **James Polk's** in his successful 1844 election. The 54°40' is the northern latitude proposed as a boundary between American and British possessions from the Rocky Mountains to Puget Sound. The slogan promised to extend the Oregon Territory to this line— deep into Canada—or go to war. Polk, needless to say, did neither, and the hollow campaign slogan was quickly irrelevant. As J. L. Dillard points out in *American Talk*, "Both Woodrow Wilson and Franklin D. Roosevelt won second terms as presidents 'who kept us out of war,' and war was declared during the second term of each."[40]

FIRESIDE CHAT. An informal address delivered over the radio to a national audience. Used to describe the thirty chats delivered by **Franklin D. Roosevelt** during the twelve years of his presidency.

On March 6, 1933, two days after his inauguration, Roosevelt declared a four-day bank holiday. Bank runs and failures had been epidemic early in the Depression, and many banks had already been closed by local action. Roosevelt suspended all banking while Congress rushed through the Emergency Banking Act on March 9, ratifying his bank holiday and providing for the reopening of many banks.

The following Sunday, March 12, FDR gave his first evening radio talk. "An Intimate Talk with the People of the United States on Banking" announced that the banks would reopen the next morning. The name *fireside chats*, used in promoting the second radio talk, was suggested by **Harry Butcher**, head of CBS's Washington office. It was first used on air by Robert Trout, who revealed in a 1984 interview that the White House had given CBS the okay to use the title in lieu of something more formal.[41]*

FDR's chats had to do primarily with the Depression and World War II. On June 5, 1944, he prepared the nation for the invasion of Europe. The next day, D-Day, he was on the radio with a prayer.

"FIRST IN WAR, FIRST IN PEACE, FIRST IN THE HEARTS OF THE AMERICAN PEOPLE." This slogan/ toast to **George Washington** was written by Major General Henry Lee III (Light-Horse Harry Lee, father of Robert E. Lee) as part of the congressional eulogy to Washington on December 26, 1799.

FIRST LADY. An honorific term for the wife of the president, commonly stated as "first lady of the land" in early citations. The *Dictionary of American English* contains an entry for *presidentess*—an early alternate term for the president's wife.

---

*FDR spoke from a table that Butcher had purchased for $15 and into which he had drilled holes to accommodate the microphones needed to broadcast the chats.

On July 12, 1849, Dolley Madison died. President **Zachary Taylor** is reputed to have eulogized the wife of the fourth president by saying, "She will never be forgotten because she was truly our First Lady for a half-century." This seems to be the first use of the term in an American context and as a specific reference to the wife of the president.

Taylor's daughter, Betty Taylor Bliss, assumed the duties of first lady upon his inauguration, as his wife had become an invalid and was confined to second floor of the White House.

Abraham Lincoln's wife, Mary, was called first lady; William Howard Russell mentioned in *My Diary North and South* (1863) "some charming little pieces of gossip about 'the First Lady in the Land.'" So was Rutherford Hayes's wife, Lucy.

The term became even more popular in 1911 when Charles Nirdlinger's comedy about Dolley Madison titled *The First Lady of the Land* opened on Broadway.

Jacqueline Kennedy, however, disapproved of the title because she claimed it made her sound like a "saddle horse."[42]

FLOOGIE BIRD. A noun of deprecation used and popularized by **Harry Truman** at the Jefferson-Jackson Day Dinner in Washington, D.C., on February 19, 1948: "These men who live in the past remind me of a toy . . . a small wooden bird called the 'Floogie Bird.' Around the Floogie Bird's neck is a label reading: "I fly backwards. I don't care where I'm going. I just want to see where I've been."

FOUNDING FATHERS. Collective name for American statesmen of the Revolutionary period, especially members of the American Constitutional Convention of 1787. The term was created by **Warren G. Harding** in 1918 as a U.S. senator and used during his 1920 "front porch" campaign.

Before Harding, the collective noun for the men who wrote the Constitution was the *framers* or the *framers of the Constitution.* An article in *American Heritage* titled "Of Deathless Remarks . . ." said that the Harding quotation was "the first use of the phrase that the combined efforts of the experts at the Library of Congress have been able to find."

The coinage occurred in Senator Harding's remarks before the Sons and Daughters of the Revolution, Washington, D.C., February 22, 1918, which included this sentence: "It is good to meet and drink at the fountains of wisdom inherited from the founding fathers of the Republic." He used it again later the same year on November 2, in a speech alleging that President Wilson was bypassing the role of the Congress in postwar plans for the country: "To say we question his plans for peace and the vitally necessary restoration which must follow is quite the truth. We want Congress to control. That was the intent of the founding fathers."

The discovery was later affirmed in a letter to the *New York Times* on August 12, 1987, by the writer Jerome Agel and reaffirmed by William Safire in his "On Language" column in the same newspaper on May 7, 1988, when he pointed out that *founding father* took hold as if it had always been with us. Safire added that Harding had an aptitude for alliteration ("not nostrums but normalcy") from which this construction sprung. Or, as he added later in his *Political Dictionary*: "'Founding Fathers' functioned as the fulfillment of his forensic fancy." *

Once Harding's 1920 campaign began, he used it often and in the context of American stability in an unstable world: "Let's hold fast to that which has come to us from the founding fathers, from the union, from those who awakened us to a little finer conscience, then get off this detour on the right track again and go ahead."[43]

The use of the term grew slowly but then got a major boost in 1941 with the publication of the book *Founding Fathers: Men Who Shaped Our Tradition* by Kenneth Umbreit. *A Dictionary of Americanisms* lists Umbreit's book as the first citation for the term.

FOUR FREEDOMS. President **Franklin D. Roosevelt** announced in his State of the Union message to the Congress, January 6, 1941: "In the future days, which we seek to make secure, we look forward to a world founded upon four essential human freedoms. The first is freedom of speech and expression—everywhere in the world. The second is freedom of every person to worship God in his own way—everywhere in the world. The third is freedom from want—which, translated into world terms, means economic understandings which will secure to every nation a healthy peacetime life for its inhabitants—everywhere in the world. The fourth is freedom from fear—which, translated into world terms, means a world-wide reduction of

---

*Safire himself was an apostle of alliteration, responsible for Spiro Agnew's famous "nattering nabobs of negativism."

armaments to such a point and in such a thorough fashion that no nation will be in a position to commit an act of physical aggression against any neighbor—anywhere in the world."

Roosevelt's speechwriter and biographer Robert E. Sherwood later attested to the fact that the four freedoms were entirely created by Roosevelt and not the product of any speechwriter.[44] *

FRAZZLE. Cause to feel completely exhausted; wear out; the state of being completely exhausted or worn out. In October 1910, **Teddy Roosevelt** said that he would beat his opponents to a frazzle, and the next day he told the press, "You may recall that I said frazzled and you may quote me on that." To Roosevelt, that was his "Frazzle speech." In 1912, he was asked if his hat was again in the ring. He demurred, but he commented on his role as phrasemaker, comparing his use of "hat in the ring" to his Frazzle speech. He said, "That phrase went broadcast"— meaning it gathered wide popular attention.[45]

Again, Roosevelt took an ordinary slang expression—albeit not one in common use—and popularized it and made it his own. *Frazzle* was recorded by *Merriam-Webster* as first showing up in 1825 as an alteration of English dialect *fazle*, to tangle or fray.

FRONT PORCH CAMPAIGN. Candidate **Warren G. Harding**'s front porch campaign during the late summer and

---

*A plaque in the stairwell of the pedestal of the Statue of Liberty is inscribed: "Liberty is the air America breathes . . . In the future days, which we seek to make secure, we look forward to a world founded upon four essential freedoms . . . freedom of speech and expression . . . freedom of worship . . . freedom from want . . . freedom from fear."

fall of 1920 captured the imagination of the country. Not only was it the first campaign to be heavily covered by the press and to receive widespread newsreel coverage, but it was also the first modern campaign to use the power of Hollywood and Broadway stars, who traveled to Marion, Ohio, for photo opportunities with Harding and his wife. Al Jolson, Lillian Russell, Douglas Fairbanks, and Mary Pickford were among the luminaries to make the pilgrimage to his front porch. Business icons Thomas Edison, Henry Ford, and Harvey Firestone also lent their support to Harding. From the onset of the campaign until the November election, more than six hundred thousand people traveled to Marion to participate.

"FULL DINNER PAIL." Motto of **William McKinley's** 1900 Republican campaign for the presidency. A dinner pail was common then: a handled pail or bucket with a removable top in which schoolchildren, laborers, and others once carried their noon meals. Every Republican parade featured a horse-drawn float, atop which was an immense replica of a dinner pail. McKinley's opponent, William Jennings Bryan, mocked the dinner pail, saying that it assumed Americans were "gluttons" who could be won over only by way of their stomachs.[46]

G

GAG RULE. Popular name for a ruling first adopted by the House of Representatives in May 1836, renewed in subsequent years, and made part of the standing orders of the House from 1840 to 1844, stating that petitions relating to slavery should be laid aside without being read aloud, debated, printed, or referred to committee. Evidence strongly suggests that the sixth president, **John Quincy Adams**, created this term in 1840 after his presidency as a member of the House of Representatives, where he fought to prevent the expansion of slavery: "I enquired . . . if the slavery resolutions of [Robert Barnwell] Rhett, and [Simeon H.] Anderson, of Kentucky were within the recent gag-rule."[47] (Both Rhett and Anderson were pro-slavery.)

GAMALIELESE. **Warren G. Harding**'s style of speech, which his critics said was overblown and riddled with puffed-up platitudes—painful to read and harder to listen to. "Here is a temple of liberty no storms may shake, here are altars of freedom no passions shall destroy," Harding said of America in a 1920 campaign speech. **H. L. Mencken** listened to Harding's inaugural address and wrote in the *Baltimore Sun* in an article titled "Gamalielese": "I rise to pay my small tribute to Dr. Harding. Setting aside a college professor or two and a half dozen dipsomaniacal newspaper reporters, he takes the first place in my Valhalla of literati. That is to say, he writes the worst English that I have ever encountered. It reminds me of a string of wet sponges; it reminds me of tattered washing on the line; it reminds me of stale bean-soup, of college yells, of dogs barking idiotically through endless nights. It is so bad that a sort of grandeur creeps into it. It drags itself out of the dark abysm (I was about to write abscess!) of pish, and crawls insanely up to the topmost pinnacle of posh. It is rumble and bumble. It is flap and doodle. It is balder and dash."[48]

Mencken was not alone. After Harding's death, the poet e. e. cummings eulogized him as "the only man, woman or child who wrote a simple declarative sentence with seven grammatical errors."

-GATE. Suffix attached to any word to denote a scandal (and usually an attempted cover-up). It originated in 1973, after the June 1972 break-in at the national headquarters of the Democratic Party at the Watergate complex by operatives working for the staff and reelection campaign of President **Richard Nixon**. As Hugh Rawson points out in "The Words of Watergate," "Almost every administration since Mr. Nixon's has had one or more -gates. A random sampling: the Ford administration's Koreagate, Carter's Billygate and Lancegate, Reagan and Bush's Irangate (also called armsgate and contragate). Bill Clinton has survived, so far, travelgate, Whitewatergate, and, most recently, Indogate (involving campaign contributions from Indonesia)."*

"GIVE 'EM HELL, HARRY." Motto given to **Harry Truman** based on a comment he made at the beginning of the western portion of a 1948 whistle-stop tour. The morning Truman left on the tour, Senator Alben Barkley, his running mate, came down to the train station to wish the president well.

"Go out there and mow 'em down," Barkley said.

"I'll mow 'em down, Alben," Truman replied, "and I'll give 'em hell."

Reporters who heard the exchange used it in their stories, and by the time Truman reached the West Coast, the crowds were shouting "Give 'em hell, Harry."

That he did. He called the Republicans "tools of the most reactionary elements," silent and cunning men "who would skim the cream from our natural resources to satisfy their own greed . . . who would tear our country apart . . . bloodsuckers with offices in Wall Street, princes of privilege, plunderers."[49]

---

*A collector on Wikipedia has amassed around 113 -gates of which, at the moment this book went to press, the most recent example was bountygate. Revealed in March 2012, it involved a number of professional football players in the employ of the New Orleans Saints as defensive players who illegally received financial rewards for big plays, including those that injured offensive players.

GLOBALONEY. Nonsensical or absurd talk or ideas concerning global issues. The word was coined on February 9, 1943, by Representative **Clare Boothe Luce** in response to the postwar thoughts of Vice President **Henry Wallace**: "Much of what Mr. Wallace calls his global thinking is, no matter how you slice it, still 'globaloney.' Mr. Wallace's warp of sense and his woof of nonsense is very tricky cloth out of which to cut the pattern of a post-war world."[50]

GOOD NEIGHBOR POLICY. Policy created by President **Franklin D. Roosevelt** in his first inaugural address on March 4, 1933. Roosevelt publicly stated for the first time the essence of the fair rule in international conduct, happily adopted by the new administration in Washington. It was a memorable occasion in the annals of hemispheric relations, said the new president: "In the field of world policy I would dedicate this nation to the policy of the good neighbor—the neighbor who resolutely respects himself and, because he does so, respects the rights of others—the neighbor who respects his obligations and respects the sanctity of his agreements in and with a world of neighbors."

It had echoes dating back to George Washington who, in his Farewell to the American People, called for "just and amicable feelings" toward all nations.

"GOOD TO THE LAST DROP." Advertising slogan. Joel Owsley Cheek was the inventor of Maxwell House Coffee, the blend that became so popular it made Nashville the center of the nation's coffee business in the early twentieth century. In

1892, he developed a recipe for a blend of premium beans and convinced the manager of the Maxwell House Hotel to try the coffee and then to serve it exclusively. The coffee was so well received by the hotel's guests that the owner gave Cheek permission to use the Maxwell House name for the coffee. The phrase "good to the last drop" was said to have been coined by President **Theodore Roosevelt** after he sipped coffee during a visit to Andrew Jackson's estate, the Hermitage, on October 21, 1907. No contemporary account of this incident survives, but the Theodore Roosevelt Association makes this statement on its website: "The Hermitage origin was attested to by a college student who witnessed it, and who went on to become president of the Tennessee state historical society." Barry Popik, the eminent lexicographer and word-history sleuth, has pointed out that "the similar slogan, 'The Last Drop Is As Good As The First,' was used by Renne's magic oil (1870), Hires root beer (1892) and Baker's hot cocoa (1910). The 'Good To The Last Drop' slogan had been used prior to 1907 by mineral spring waters (1865), root beer (1900), Challenge Blend coffee (1903), beer (1904) and Woman's Club coffee (1905)."[51]

GREAT SOCIETY. A set of domestic programs announced by **Lyndon Johnson**. The name was suggested by his speechwriter, Richard Goodwin.

GREAT WHITE FLEET. At the direction of President **Theodore Roosevelt**, sixteen new battleships and four destroyers of the Atlantic Fleet were sent around the world between December 16, 1907, and February 22, 1909, as a show of American

sea power. The ships were painted white and embellished with gilded scrollwork on their bows. The Atlantic Fleet battleships later came to be known as the Great White Fleet.

As Elizabeth Webber and Mike Feinsilber point out in *Grand Allusions: A Lively Guide to Those Expressions, Terms, and References You Ought to Know but Might Not*, "The phrase is now invoked in descriptions of contemporary flexings of American Naval muscle."[52]

GULF STREAM. A current of warm water arching northerly and easterly from the Gulf of Mexico toward Europe. Benjamin Franklin, deputy postmaster, wondered why it took packet ships (which carried mail) longer to sail from England to New York than it took merchant ships to travel west to east. He asked his cousin, Timothy Folger, a Nantucket whaling captain, to explain this conundrum. Folger told Franklin that the merchant ships identified this warm, swift water by the bubbles on the surface of the ocean from undersea whales and sailed with it, whereas the packet ships sailed against it. In 1769, **Benjamin Franklin** prepared and published the first chart of the ocean current, and named it the Gulf Stream. The poet and lexicographer John Ciardi wrote in his *Second Browser's Dictionary, and Native's Guide to the Unknown American Language*,

"The name now strikes us as inevitable as if from nature itself. I take that fact, too, as evidence of Franklin's genius. A more pretentious man might, in the current academic manner, have called it 'the northeasterly arc of the pelagic confluence.'"[53]

HATCHET MAN. A trailblazer or axe man serving in a military unit. At the beginning of the French and Indian War (1754–1763), African Americans were not allowed in Virginia's militia. But when faced with a severe shortage of manpower, free blacks were permitted to serve in menial capacities. The term first appeared in 1755 in a letter from **George Washington** to Colonel Peter Hog of the Virginia Regiment: "I think it will be advisable to detain both mulattoes and negroes in your company, and employ them as Pioneers or Hatchetmen" to clear the route of trees, rocks, and other obstacles. According to *A Dictionary of Americanisms*, in 1889, the term was first used to describe organized bands of Chinese criminals who commit murder for pay—with the clear implications that the weapon of choice is the hatchet.

The modern use of the word *hatchet man*, as applied to a person, especially a journalist, employed to attack and destroy another person's reputation, did not come along until 1944, when it made its debut in *Time* magazine. In 1949, "Truman's Hatchetmen" was used, according to *A Dictionary of Americanisms*, to describe organizing groups sent through the South to work for the defeat of those opposing his pro-labor legislative programs.[54]

HEARTS AND MINDS. This term came into currency during the Vietnam War. **Lyndon Johnson** invoked the phrase in 1965 when he said, "We must be ready to fight in Vietnam, but the ultimate victory will depend on the hearts and minds of the people who actually live out there." In his *Political Dictionary*, William Safire attributes the phrase to **Theodore Roosevelt**, who explained his popularity to his young aide Douglas MacArthur this way: I "put into words what is in their hearts and minds but not in their mouths." However, James S. Olson in *Dictionary of the Vietnam War* attributes it in reversed form to **John Adams** in his description of the Revolutionary War: "The Revolution was effected before the war was commenced. The Revolution was in the minds and hearts of the people."[55]

HOOVERIZE. To be sparing or economical, especially in the use of food. It stems from **Herbert Hoover's** role as U.S. food commissioner during World War I. According to the *New York Tribune*, "It is now assured that Mr. Hoover is about to become our food regulator . . . and since he has . . . exhorted the public to exercise the utmost economy in the use of foodstuffs . . . I suggest that 'to Hooverize' be universally adopted as expressing the assistance every one of us . . . can render in that direction."[56]

HOOVERVILLE. A makeshift village of cheap tin and cardboard shanties and shacks that people during the Great Depression were forced to live in. It was named for **Herbert Hoover,** president at the time. The word made its published debut, according to Mitford Mathews in his *Dictionary of Americanisms*, in the *New Republic* of May 24, 1933: "Hoovervilles are in a separate nation, with separate codes, though the men who live in them are still subject to a sort of imperialist intervention."

HOTLINE. A direct telephone line set up for a specific purpose, especially for use in emergencies or for communication between heads of government. This word began to appear in the popular press as early as 1954 to describe the call over a dedicated telephone line between the White House and the Strategic Air Command that would initiate war with the Soviet Union: "If the Russians ever trespass too far, the Air Force will act. A code word, spoken over the 'hot line' from the Command Post in Washington to the Strategic Air Command in Omaha, will light the fuse under Moscow." But the word did not achieve major status until 1963 in the wake of the previous year's Cuban Missile Crisis, after

Jess Gorkin of *Parade* magazine proposed the idea of a direct link between the White House and the Kremlin.[57]

On August 30, 1963, the **John F. Kennedy** White House issued a statement that the new hotline would "help reduce the risk of war occurring by accident or miscalculation." Instead of relying on telegrammed letters that had to travel overseas, the new technology was a momentous step toward the very near future when American and Soviet leaders could simply pick up the phone and be instantly connected twenty-four hours a day, seven days a week. It was agreed that the line would be used only in emergencies, not for more routine governmental exchanges.

Although it was Gorkin's idea and he was the first to apply the term, JFK's name became associated with the red telephone hotline that linked the White House and the Kremlin.

"A HOUSE DIVIDED AGAINST ITSELF CANNOT STAND." Perhaps **Abraham Lincoln**'s most enduring metaphor for America, included in a speech delivered at the close of the Republican state convention that named him the candidate for the U.S. Senate, in Springfield, Illinois, June 16, 1858. He said, "We are now far into the fifth year, since a policy was initiated, with the avowed object, and confident promise, of putting an end to slavery agitation. Under the operation of that policy, that agitation has not only, not ceased, but has constantly augmented. In my opinion, it will not cease, until a crisis shall have been reached, and passed. A house divided against itself cannot stand. I believe this government cannot endure, permanently half slave and half free. I do not expect the Union to be dissolved—I do not expect the house to fall—but I do expect it will cease to be divided. It will become all one thing, or all the other."[58]

Friends and political allies thought the remarks made that day were political suicide. The words that Lincoln made famous are a slight paraphrase of "And if a house be divided against itself, that house cannot stand" (Mark 3:25).

HUSTLING. Jostling or moving rapidly. The first evidence of this word being used is in a 1760 entry in **John Adams**'s diary: "Wasted the day with a magazine in my hand . . . I had no conveniences or companions for pleasure, either in walking, riding, drinking, hustling, or any thing else."[59]

HYPHENATED AMERICANS. A disparaging term made popular by **Theodore Roosevelt** for those who regarded themselves as, in his words, "50-50 Americans" and were possessed of a dual loyalty. The term appeared as early as 1893, according to J. S. Farmer and W. E. Henley in *Slang III*, but it did not gain much attention until Roosevelt used it as a synonym for those with divided loyalties.

"There is no room in this country for hyphenated Americanism," Roosevelt said in a speech to the Knights of Columbus at Carnegie Hall in New York on Columbus Day 1915. "When I refer to hyphenated Americans I do not refer to naturalized Americans. Some of the very best Americans I have ever known were naturalized Americans born abroad. But a hyphenated American is not an American at all . . . The one absolutely certain way of bringing this nation to ruin, of preventing all possibility of it continuing to be a nation at all, would be to permit it to become a tangle of squabbling nationalities, an intricate knot of German-Americans, Irish-Americans, English-Americans, French-Americans, Scandinavian-Americans, or Italian-Americans, each preserving its separate nationality, each at heart feeling more sympathy with Europeans of that nationality than with the other citizens of the American Republic . . . There is no such thing as a hyphenated American who is a good American. The only man who is a good American is the man who is an American and nothing else."[60]

President **Woodrow Wilson** regarded "hyphenated Americans" with suspicion, noting in an address on the League of Nations, "Any man who carries a hyphen about with him carries a dagger that he is ready to plunge into the vitals of this Republic whenever he gets ready."

"I DO NOT CHOOSE TO RUN." On August 2, 1927, while residing in his summerhouse in the Black Hills of South Dakota, incumbent president **Calvin Coolidge** told his secretary, Everett Sanders, "Now—I am not going to run for president. If I should serve as president again, I should serve almost ten years, which is too long for a president in this country." He handed Sanders his statement: "I do not choose to run for president in 1928." Coolidge was a succinct speaker, but this ambiguous statement was variously interpreted throughout the country. As the *New York Times* recalled in Coolidge's obituary, in which discussion of the decision took a major part, "Many saw in it a sincere wish for retirement, but still a willingness to accept the nomination should an insistent demand arise. Others looked upon it as a final decision that he would not be a candidate for re-election. There were many, too, who regarded it as a shrewd attempt to avoid the third term issue by having himself 'drafted for office.'"

A "draft Coolidge" movement took place, and Coolidge

himself had to eliminate himself entirely in an address before the Republican National Committee the following December.

But the draft Coolidge movement could not be stopped. When the Republican National Convention met in Kansas City in June 1928, so many influential leaders of state delegations were preparing to vote for him that the president sent Everett Sanders from his summer camp in Wisconsin to Kansas City to notify those leaders to vote for anybody else. It was not his doing, he wrote after leaving the presidency, that they turned to Herbert Hoover.

Later Coolidge wrote, "While I had a desire to be relieved of the pretensions and delusions of public life, it was not because of any attraction of pleasure or idleness. We draw our Presidents from the people. It is a wholesome thing for them to return to the people. I came from them. I wish to be one of them."[61]

"I KNOW ONLY TWO TUNES, ONE OF THEM IS 'YANKEE DOODLE' AND THE OTHER ISN'T." **Ulysses S. Grant** had the ability to deliver memorable lines. Commenting on the short-range infantry muskets used during the Mexican War, he said, "A man might fire at you all day without your finding it out."

"I LIKE IKE." This 1952 campaign slogan for **Dwight D. Eisenhower** helped to propel the Republican general who had commanded Allied forces in World War II into the White

House. It also became "one of the most well-known and catchiest political slogans of all time."

"IF YOU CAN'T STAND THE HEAT, GET OUT OF THE KITCHEN." An aphorism coined by **Harry Truman** to suggest that if you can't cope, you should leave the work to someone who can. Truman is known to have used it at least as early as 1942, before becoming president. Here's an example from an Idaho newspaper, the *Soda Springs Sun,* from July of that year: "Favorite rejoinder of Senator Harry S. Truman, when a member of his war contracts investigating committee objects to his strenuous pace: 'If you don't like the heat, get out of the kitchen.'"[62]

IFFY. Describing a question, proposal, prospect, or decision that is full of "ifs"; something that is contingent, doubtful. This adjective is the invention of **Franklin D. Roosevelt,** who began using it early in his administration. By May 9, 1937, *This Week* magazine could carry this line: "Very 'iffy,' Mr. Roosevelt might characterize such talk." The *Chicago Daily News* on January 17, 1941, for example, agreed: "The President had been asked the status of some proposal, or of some event . . . whether this event was likely to happen . . . The president replied that the whole thing was 'iffy.'"

For many years, whenever the word was used, it was still attributed to FDR. "I am going to write what President Roosevelt would have called a very iffy column," wrote the television critic John Crosby in the *Washington Post.*[63]

INDECIPHERABLE. Incapable of being deciphered or made out. **Thomas Jefferson** used the word in an 1802 letter to Robert Livingston, the U.S. minister to France: "I am sending you a cipher to be used between us, which will give you some trouble to understand, but, once understood, it is the easiest to use, the most indecipherable . . ." Jefferson was referring to a cipher devised by the mathematician and philosopher Robert Patterson. He and Jefferson regularly exchanged coded correspondence. The coinage can be seen as a logical progression in Jefferson's correspondence with Patterson, who noted in a letter to Jefferson the previous Christmas that "a perfect cipher"—or code system—should, among other things, "be absolutely inscrutable to all unacquainted with the particular key or secret for deciphering."[64]

INDIANIAN. Demonym created in 1784 by **Thomas Jefferson** for a resident of Indiana. He wrote to James Madison: "Should we not be the first movers, and the Indianians and Kentuckians take themselves off and claim to the Alleghany, I am afraid Congress would secretly wish them well." The word was largely abandoned for the more usual Indianan and the dominant Hoosier. Indiana became a state in 1816.[65]

INDOORS. Within doors; not outdoors. **George Washington**, writing in 1899: "There are many sorts of in-doors work, which can be executed in Hail, Rain, or Snow, as well as in sunshine."[66]

INFORMATION SUPERHIGHWAY. The global information and communications network that includes the Internet and other networks and switching systems. A metaphor that was popularized but not, as many have claimed, coined by Senator and later Vice President **Al Gore** beginning in 1991 as a piece of political rhetoric to capture the imagination of the U.S. electorate. By his own account, the term was partly inspired by the work of his father, a U.S. senator who was involved in the construction of the national highway system. By far, one of the most hackneyed metaphors of the 1990s, it begat such terms as "information highway," "infobahn," and "I-way," as well as a number of spin-offs, applied to traffic on the World Wide Web including "on-ramps," "traffic jams," "tollbooths," and (my favorite) "roadkill on the Information Superhighway."

INFRACT. To interfere with. **George Washington** asserted that all nations had a right to their preferred form of government, "provided it *infracts* no right or is not dangerous to others." *Infract* appears a number of times in **Alexander Hamilton**'s political writings, but it never caught on. Nor did Hamilton's invention, *to retrospect*, although it sounds like just the sort of word that a modern politician would appreciate.

INNOCUOUS DESUETUDE. A whimsical euphemism for prolonged discontinuance, created by **Grover Cleveland** in a message to Congress in 1886: "After an existence of nearly twenty years of almost innocuous desuetude, these laws are brought forth."

INSTANT ANALYSIS. A term coined by Vice President **Spiro Agnew** in 1969 to refer to the practice of summarizing and commenting on an important White House speech immediately after the speaker has gone off the air. Four years after the criticism was leveled, the Columbia Broadcasting System banned the practice for presidential broadcasts for five months before it was discontinued.[67]

INSTANT PRESIDENT. Self-deprecating description that **Gerald Ford** applied to himself after taking office without being elected: "I was America's first instant Vice President—and now, America's first instant President. The Marine Corps Band is so confused, they don't know whether to play 'Hail to the Chief' or 'You've Come a Long Way, Baby.'"

INVISIBLE GOVERNMENT. **Theodore Roosevelt**'s coinage for the corrupt alliance of business and politics. "Behind the ostensible Government sits enthroned an invisible Government, owing no allegiance and acknowledging no responsibility to the people. To destroy this invisible Government, to befoul the unholy alliance between corrupt business and corrupt politics, is the first task of the statesmanship of the day . . . This country belongs to the people. Its resources, its business, its laws, its institutions, should be utilized, maintained, or altered in whatever manner will best promote the general interest."[68]

"IT'S THE ECONOMY, STUPID." James Carville, a strategist for **Bill Clin-**

ton's 1992 presidential campaign, hung a sign saying, "The economy, stupid," at the Little Rock campaign headquarters. It was a reminder that no matter what other topics the George H. W. Bush campaign focused on, this was the overriding issue. Clinton used the catchphrase "It's the economy, stupid," and the electorate agreed.

JABBLE. To shake or mix up together; to shake up or cause to splash through agitation. This onomatopoetic word first appears in **George Washington**'s diary entry of April 14, 1760, in his "recipe" for mixing compost: "All [the above-mentioned "ingredients," including earth, sand, mud, clay, and horse, sheep, and cow dung] mix'd . . . in the most effectual manner by reducing the whole to a tolerable degree of fineness and jabling them well together in a Cloth." In *Presidential Voices*, Allan Metcalf notes that Washington's *jabble* is an example of how presidential use does not guarantee the success of a word. "We just don't jabble much nowadays."[69]

JACK. Soon after he was elected in 1960, **John F. Kennedy** let it be known that he did not want to be known publicly as Jack, a request that the press honored to the extent that a *New York Times Magazine* article on nicknames referred to him as "J—k." Kennedy's Secret Service code name was Lancer, a possible allusion to Camelot.

JACKSON. The name of the seventh president, **Andrew Jackson**, used as a modifier. Jackson's most direct contribution to the vocabulary of his time was the lending of his name as an attribute. As Mary Helen Dohan writes in *Our Own Words*, "It occurred in so many combinations—Jackson men, Jackson party, Jackson banks, Jackson money (gold), Jackson coats, hats, jackets, trousers, shoes, slippers—that the *Albany Evening Journal* of August 8, 1834, complained that the rage for naming everything after Jackson was evidence of his 'bloated reputation.'" The *Dictionary of American English* lists Jackson Crackers as a name for firecrackers.[70]

JACKSONIAN. Pertaining to or characteristic of **Andrew Jackson**; a follower of Jackson.

JACKSONIANA. Name proposed in 1841 in the Tennessee Senate for a state lying to the west of the Tennessee River to be carved out of portions of Kentucky, Mississippi, and Tennessee in honor of **Andrew Jackson**.

JACKSONISM. Belief system based on the political and social ideas of **Andrew Jackson**, which included the extension of voting rights beyond the moneyed class and support of homesteaders enlarging the United States.

JACKSONIZE. An archaic term (active ca. 1829–1937) "to defeat (severely) in battle," from **Andrew Jackson**'s reputation as a fighter, especially at the Battle of New Orleans.

JEFFERSONIAN. Of or pertaining to the politics and policies of **Thomas Jefferson**. There are a number of special combinations for Jeffersonian, which appear in *A Dictionary of American English* and elsewhere, including a system of library management called *Jeffersonian classification* and a condition of *Jeffersonian simplicity* marked by the absence of ceremony in political and social matters.[71]

JEFFERSONIANISM. Political principles and ideas of **Thomas Jefferson**, which include a staunch belief in separation of church and state, states' rights, an agrarian economy, and civil liberties (in contrast to *Hamiltonianism*).

JEFFERSONITE. A greenish-black variety of pyroxene, containing some zinc and manganese. Named in 1822 after President **Thomas Jefferson** and perhaps the only mineral named for a U.S. president.

JEFFERSON'S MANUAL. Popular name for *Manual of Parliamentary Practice for the Use of the Senate of the United States* (1801) by Thomas Jefferson.

JIMMY. **Jimmy Carter** insisted that the diminutive form of his name be used at all times—as opposed to James Earl. Many people put a spin on it, and *Jimmy* came out as the mock-Georgian "Gym-ma." William Safire points out in his *Political Dictionary* that Carter was the first president to insist on the diminutive. On the other hand, the Harry of Harry S Truman's name was his real name and not a nickname. S (without a period) was his full middle name: "I was supposed to be named

Harrison Shippe Truman, taking the middle name from my paternal grandfather. Others in my family wanted my middle name to be Solomon, taken from my maternal grandfather. But apparently no agreement could be reached and my name was recorded and stands simply as Harry S Truman." (He was sometimes called "Harry 'S for nothing' Truman.")

"KEEP THE BALL ROLLING."
During the presidential campaign of 1840, an immense steel-ribbed ball covered in canvas and plastered with this and other slogans was pushed from town to town in support of **William Henry Harrison**, thereby popularizing the expression. As they  rolled the ball, supporters chanted this pro–Harrison-Tyler and anti–Van Buren ditty:

> *What has caused this great commotion, motion, motion,*
> *Our country through?*
> *It is the ball a-rolling on,*
> *For Tippecanoe and Tyler too, Tippecanoe and Tyler too.*
> *And with them we'll beat the little Van, Van, Van;*
> *Van is a used-up man,*
> *And with them we'll beat little Van.*[72]

KITCHEN CABINET. A coterie of personal unofficial advisers to the president, popularly believed to have greater influence than the actual cabinet (or the elected representatives, etc.). The term was applied first to the presidency of **Andrew Jackson** (1829–1837) and started showing up in print in 1832. In search of ideas and opinions, Jackson would convene a group of political and nonpolitical allies in the back room of the White House. There, they'd talk about the issues the nation faced and what to do about them. As H. W. Brands wrote in *Andrew Jackson: His Life and Times*, "Unlike every previous president except Washington, Jackson had almost no intimates in the national capital upon his inauguration . . . Jackson knew his cabinet secretaries, other than [Secretary of War John Henry] Eaton, by reputation alone. For this reason he turned for advice to men whose judgment and loyalty he had learned to trust during the long campaign. William Lewis of Tennessee stood first among the equals. Amos Kendall, an ardently pro-Jackson editor from Kentucky, came next. Duff Green, a Missouri transplant who now edited the fiercely Jacksonian *United States Telegraph* at Washington, and Isaac Hill, for years a lonely Jacksonian in New Hampshire, rounded out the clique. Andrew Donelson, the president's nephew, surrogate son, and now personal secretary, was an ex officio member of the group."

Critics concentrated their fire against the "kitchen cabinet," as they derisively called Jackson's informal circle. Lewis was assailed as the president's personal propagandist, while Kendall, Green, and Hill were branded hack writers remarkable only for their singular prejudice for all things Jacksonian. Even some of Jackson's friends acknowledged that appearances weren't good. "We lament to see so many of the editorial corps favored with the patronage of the Administration," Thomas Ritchie wrote to Martin Van Buren. Ritchie edited the *Richmond Enquirer* and had backed Jackson strongly, although not as strongly as Kendall, Green, and Hill. When W. S. Archer, a Jackson supporter, was being considered for the post of minister to England, he said that he could be persuaded to accept only "if there be no other mode of preventing its being given to the most despicable of all the Protegees of the Kitchen Cabinet."[73]

"LAW AND ORDER CANDIDATE." The term "law and order" did not originate with **Calvin Coolidge**, but he was the first to base a political campaign on being an apostle of the concept. It began with his role as Massachusetts governor  in putting down the 1919 Boston police strike. "There is no right to strike against the public safety by anybody, anywhere, anytime" was his mantra while maintaining his promise of law and order. The *New York Times'* report on his reelection as governor was headlined, "A Triumph for Law and Order."

When an attempt was made to nominate Coolidge as the Republican presidential candidate in 1920, his supporters compiled a collection of his speeches called *Law and Order* and carried banners with the same message. Coolidge was nominated for vice president under the standard-bearer Warren G. Harding.[74]

LEGALIZED LARCENY. Term coined by **Calvin Coolidge** in his 1925 inaugural address in discussing tax reduction. "The collection of any taxes which are not absolutely required, which do not beyond reasonable doubt contribute to the public welfare, is only a species of legalized larceny."[75]

LENGTHILY. At length; fully. **Thomas Jefferson** created this adverb in 1787. "As to the new Constitution I find myself nearly a Neutral. There is a great mass of good in it, . . . but there is also to me a bitter pill, or two. I have written somewhat lengthily to Mr. Madison on this subject."[76]

LENGTHY. Long, protracted. **John Adams** is credited with first deploying this adjective in a diary entry of January 3, 1759, in which he had written a sermon addressed to himself: "Which, dear Youth, will you prefer? A Life of Effeminacy, Indolence and obscurity, or a Life of Industry, Temperance, and Honour?" After several hundred such words, Adams ended, "I grow too minute and lengthy."

According to Thomas Pyles in *Words and Ways of American English, lengthy* is a word of seventeenth-century origin given widespread respectability by Adams, Thomas Jefferson, and Alexander Hamilton. Pyles notes, "It was for some time a particularly sharp thorn in the side of British commentators." In any case, the *Oxford English Dictionary* gives Adams the nod as the first to use the term in a surviving document.[77]

LINCOLNDOM. During the Civil War, a Southern nickname for the North. The opposing nickname for the Confederate States was Dixie.

LINCOLNESQUE. A word from 1894 that has come to refer to someone who is (1) tall and gawky, (2) full-bearded, (3) both of the above.

LINCOLNIAN. Characteristic of Abraham Lincoln.

LINCOLNIANA. Books, letters, and relics relating to Lincoln.

LINCOLNITE. A believer in the political principles and politics of Abraham Lincoln; a Union soldier or sympathizer during the Civil War.

LITTLE BROWN BROTHERS. During the U.S. occupation of the Philippines, a paternalistic American reference to Filipinos by **William Howard Taft.** In 1900, Taft entered politics on an international level when he accepted the position of the first civil governor of the Philippine Islands, which two years earlier had been acquired by the United States as a result of the Spanish-American War. He was asked to serve by President McKinley. Taft excelled as governor of the Philippines and gained great respect and popularity among the population, whom he called "my little brown brothers." Under Taft, the Philippines became a model of enlightened colonial government. Despite the fact that Taft desired a place on the U.S. Supreme Court, he twice turned down an appointment to the Court in order to stay in the Philippines. (After his presidency, he finally got his wish in 1921, when President Warren Harding appointed him chief justice; he served on the Court until 1930.)

LOOSE CANNON. A person or thing that is unpredictable, uncontrollable, and highly destructive. It alludes to the danger of an untethered muzzle-loading cannon on old-time warships, which were loaded on rolling carriages. Some years after the fact, **Theodore Roosevelt** was credited with applying the term for nautical danger to a personality quirk. William Allen White, a noted U.S. journalist and politician around the turn of the twentieth century and a close friend of Roosevelt, included in his autobiography, published soon after his death in 1944, the following reminiscence: "He [Roosevelt] said: 'I don't want to be the old cannon loose on the deck in the storm.'"[78]

LUNATIC FRINGE. A minority group of adherents to a political or other movement or set of beliefs that is at odds with mainstream belief. Coined by **Theodore Roosevelt**, who first

deployed it in his review of the International Exhibition of Modern Art, the notorious "Armory Show" of 1913 in New York City. His review read in part: "It is vitally necessary to move forward and to shake off the dead hand, often the fossilized dead hand, of the reactionaries; and yet we have to face the fact that there is apt to be a lunatic fringe among the votaries of any forward movement. In this recent art exhibition the lunatic fringe was fully in evidence, especially in the rooms devoted to the Cubists and the Futurists, or Near-Impressionists."*

Roosevelt quickly adopted the term for other uses, specifically reformers whose reforms were beyond his level of tolerance: "Among the wise and high-minded people who in self-respecting and genuine fashion strive earnestly for peace, there are the foolish fanatics always to be found in such a movement and always discrediting it—the men who form the lunatic fringe in all reform movements."[79]

A Google search of "lunatic fringe" conducted in the fall of 2012 yielded no fewer than 1,560,000 hits. A significant number of these are for the names of hairdressers.

---

*The work on view at this groundbreaking show that may have been on Roosevelt's mind was Marcel Duchamp's *Nude Descending a Staircase*.

"MA, MA, WHERE'S MY PA?" Failed presidential candidate James Blaine's supporters used this slogan to make fun of rumors (false) that his opponent, **Grover Cleveland**, had fathered an illegitimate child. After winning the election, Cleveland supporters added, "Gone to the White House, Ha, Ha, Ha," to the slogan. To their credit, Cleveland supporters also came up with this gem: "Blaine, Blaine, James G. Blaine, the Continental Liar from the State of Maine."

MALEFACTORS OF GREAT WEALTH. The word *malefactor* had been in use in English since 1438 according to the *Oxford English Dictionary* to mean a felon or criminal but beginning in 1895 **Teddy Roosevelt** began to apply it to the rich and selfish. He used the term on a number of occasion but this is how he defined them in 1917. "Too much cannot be said against the men of wealth who sacrifice everything to getting wealth. There is not in the world a more ignoble character than the mere money-getting American, insensible to every duty, regardless of every principle, bent only on amassing a fortune, and putting his fortune only to the basest uses—whether these uses be to speculate in stocks and wreck railroads himself, or to allow his son to lead a life of foolish and expensive idleness and gross debauchery, or to purchase some scoundrel of high social position, foreign or native, for his daughter. Such a man is only the more dangerous if he occasionally does some deed like founding a college or endowing a church, which makes those good people who are also foolish forget his real iniquity. These men are equally careless of the working men, whom they oppress, and of the State, whose existence they imperil. There are not very many of them, but there is a very great number of men who approach more or less closely to the type, and, just in so far as they do so approach, they are curses to the country."[80]

MAMMOTH. Comparable to the prehistoric mammoth in size; huge, gigantic. The first evidence of the word being used in this sense appears in an 1801 reference to a large veal presented to **Thomas Jefferson.** "I received . . . a present of a quarter of a Mammoth-veal which at 115 days old weighed 438 lb."[81]

MANIFEST DESTINY. The doctrine of the inevitability of Anglo-Saxon superiority, used to rationalize U.S. territorial expansion in the 1840s and 1850s. It asserted that expansion of the United States throughout the American continents was both justified and inevitable. The phrase was coined in 1845 by the U.S. journalist John L. O'Sullivan and was initially used in regard to Mexican and Indian land in Texas and the Southwest: "Our manifest destiny to overspread the continent allotted by Providence for the free development of our yearly multiplying millions." The term was appropriated and popularized by President **James Polk** as a way of disguising his intention to gather more territory—namely, extending the nation from the Atlantic to the Pacific.[82]

MARSHALL PLAN. Popular name for the United States' plan to supply financial assistance to certain Western European countries to further their recovery after the Second World War. Named for George Catlett Marshall, U.S. soldier and statesman, who proposed the European Recovery Program—its official name—in June 1947.When it came time to name the plan, presidential aide Clark Clifford suggested that it be called the Truman Plan. **Harry Truman** dismissed the idea at once, insisting it be called the Marshall Plan, adding that Marshall deserved no less. He added, "Anything that is sent up to the Senate and House with my name on it will quiver a couple of times and die."

As David McCullough points out in his biography *Truman*, "More than once in his presidency, Truman would be remembered saying it was remarkable how much could be accomplished if you didn't care who received the credit."[83]

MASON-DIXON LINE. Name for the arbitrary 233-mile boundary between Maryland and Pennsylvania, taken as the northern limit of slave-owning U.S. states before abolition. Used later to allude to the cultural and political differences between the North and the South. It was named for Charles Mason (1728–1786) and Jeremiah Dixon (1733–1779), English surveyors and astronomers who defined most of the boundary between Pennsylvania and Maryland by survey between 1763 and 1767. The Southern side of the line is Dixon's, from which

Dixie, a nickname for the Southern states, derived. The line was named by **Thomas Jefferson** in a letter of August 26, 1776, to Edmund Pendleton: "I am indebted to you for a topic to deny to the Pensylvania [*sic*] claim to a line 39 complete degrees from the equator. As an advocate I shall certainly insist on it; but I wish they would compromise by an extension of Mason & Dixon's line."[84]

MICHIGANDER. Demonym for a native or inhabitant of Michigan. The first recorded use of this word was in a speech given by **Abraham Lincoln**, then a representative of the Whigs in Congress, during the 1848 presidential campaign. Zachary Taylor (Whig), Lewis Cass (Democrat), and Martin Van Buren (Free Soil) were on the ballot. Lincoln, who backed Taylor, was especially dismissive of Cass, whom he referred to as "the great Michigander."[85]

In 1979, the state legislature voted to make *Michiganian* the official demonym. The bill was introduced at the behest of newspaper editors who were confused by a variety of names, including *Michigander, Michiganite,* and *Michiganer.* Nevertheless, some citizens continue to call themselves Michiganders. It is also the name given by H. L. Mencken in *The American Language.* However, because of the *-gander,* its prestige suffers some from those who puckishly insist, "If the men are *Michiganders,* the women are *Michigeese.*"

Michiganite is given in the U.S. Government Printing Office *Style Manual* and was put there by the office's Style Board. This word has been fought by residents for years. An article in the *Christian Science Monitor* on December 19, 1957, pointed out that there were many in the state who wished the government in Washington would leave the name alone. Robert Furlong, an executive of the Michigan Tourist Council was quoted as saying that *Michiganite* "sounds like something you'd dig out of the ground." He favored *Michiganian* because it "just plain sounds better. It has a roll and a savor to it." *Merriam-Webster's Collegiate Dictionary* includes both *Michiganite* and *Michigander.*

All of this debate over the proper name for a person from Michigan suggests a certain zaniness that was underscored in a letter from Brooklynite Lillian Tudiver: "I am sure that this is one of many letters you have received pointing out that Michiganer or Michiganah [sounds like a word that] means a crazy person in Yiddish. The word is *meshuggener*."

MILITARY-INDUSTRIAL COMPLEX. By far the most significant contribution to the American lexicon from **Dwight Eisenhower** was this phrase coined for his 1961 farewell address to describe the powerful alliance of the military, government agencies, and corporations involved in the defense industry. The military-industrial complex was seen as a danger, as each sector has an interest, either financial or strategic, in expanding the government's arms budget, which could lead to an arms race and money being diverted from more deserving enterprises. Academic experts in the think tanks, the extensive defense lobby organizations, and their political friends are also part of this self-perpetuating complex.

Eisenhower's farewell speech is the only such address with the staying power of George Washington's, which had a parallel warning. In his 1796 farewell address to the people of the United States, the first president talked of avoiding "those

overgrown military establishments which, under any form of government, are inauspicious to liberty, and which are to be regarded as particularly hostile to republican liberty." Similarly, on September 5, 1919, in a speech in St. Louis, Woodrow Wilson said, "The seed of war in the modern world is industrial and commercial rivalry. This war [World War I] . . . was a commercial and industrial war. It was not a political war."

The farewell speech was written in large part by Eisenhower's primary speechwriter, Malcolm Moos, who quite possibly is the actual phrasemaker here, but the concept is totally in keeping with Eisenhower's earlier warnings and may have been his own.

MISSION ACCOMPLISHED. Never actually stated by **George W. Bush**, but it appeared on the banner behind him when he stood on the USS *Abraham Lincoln* and declared the major war operations in Iraq to be over (May 1, 2003).

MISUNDERESTIMATE. To seriously underestimate. Created by **George W. Bush** in a speech in Bentonville, Arkansas, on November 6, 2000: "They misunderestimated me." The British novelist and journalist Philip Hensher called the term one of Bush's "most memorable additions to the language, and an incidentally expressive one: it may be that we rather needed a word for 'to underestimate by mistake.'" Bush connected himself to Thomas Jefferson in his remarks on Jefferson Day, April 12, 2001, when explaining his use of this word. He said, "Most people don't realize this, but Thomas Jefferson and I share a hobby. We both like to make up words. According to the *Oxford English Dictionary*, Mr. Jefferson contributed more new words to the language than any other U.S. president . . . The other day I tried a new word for our press corps: misunderestimate. It's not quite in Jefferson's league, but I am giving it my best shot."

"All that endless mean talk about Bushisms from media elites and academics?" asked Jennifer Harper in the *Washington Times* in 2010. "Seems like his critics misunderestimated former President George W. Bush. His memoir *Decision Points* has sold 2 million copies since it was released in November; the book is not even in paperback yet."[86]

MOLLYCODDLE. A pampered or overprotected man or boy; someone who lacks resolution, energy, or hardihood. The word had been in English since 1833 and made its literary debut in 1849 in William Makepeace Thackeray's *Pendennis*: "You have been bred up as a molly-coddle, Pen, and spoilt by the women." But it was given new life with the voice of **Theodore Roosevelt**, who railed against the condition and even went as far as to call baseball "a mollycoddle game"—as contrasted with the manly game of tennis.[87]

In 1907, Roosevelt created a stir when he applied the mollycoddle label to President Charles William Eliot of Harvard University and those who were proposing the abolition of football, basketball, and hockey, which were "fierce" contests and undesirable games for gentlemen to play in their existing state. In a speech on the campus on February 4, 1907, Roosevelt called Eliot's proposal "simple nonsense" and did not want to see the university turn out mollycoddles instead of vigorous men. Eliot responded by restating his position, adding that football encourages "the reckless spirit," and that the "excesses of cheering which characterize present intercollegiate contests are "absolutely unnatural."

It was a tempest in a teapot that generated a lot of headlines but little more. Nevertheless, TR was able to use the word and the idea as his nemesis for years to come. Here is a typical TR rant against the mollycoddle: "In the long run the 'sissy' and the 'mollycoddle' are as undesirable members of society as the crook and the bully. I don't like the crook and the bully. Don't misunderstand me; I will abate both of them when I get the chance at them. But, after all, there is the possibility that you can reform the crook or the bully, but you cannot reform the 'sissy' or the 'mollycoddle,' because there is not anything there to reform. With a nation, as with an individual, weakness, cowardice, and flabby failure to insist upon what is right, even if a certain risk comes in insisting, may be as detrimental, not only from the standpoint of the individual or the nation, but from the standpoint of humanity at large, as wickedness itself."[88]

MONOCRAT. Ruling alone; someone who favors monarchic rule. **Thomas Jefferson**'s neologism for a believer in monarchy and for the Federalists who sympathized with England rather than France: "The war between France and England has brought forward the Republicans and Monocrats in every state." It became, as Nathan Schachner wrote in his biography of Jefferson, "the most opprobrious item in his arsenal of epithets. By virtue of this distrust of all things English, Jefferson inevitably gravitated to a trust in all things French, even when the course of revolution there shifted away from the purity and generous enthusiasm of its beginning. To the end of his days, he was firmly convinced that Hamilton and his friends were intent on establishing an English-type monarch, aristocracy, and English-type institutions in this country; and that it was only because of the unremitting efforts of himself and his friends that that intent had not been translated into action."

Monocrat did not die with Jefferson—albeit the word was used less and less over time. In 1952, when Theodore McKeldin ran against (and defeated) Dr. H. C. "Curley" Byrd for governor of Maryland, he called him "an autocrat," a "sceptered hermit," "an absolute monocrat," and "a power-hungry campus conspirator." (Byrd was at the time the president of the University of Maryland.)[89]

MONROE DOCTRINE. The principle, doctrine, or policy, established by **James Monroe**, of regarding any attempt by a European power to gain control of territory in North or South America (whether by settlement, purchase, or aggression) as an unfriendly act. The principle, or series of principles, as put forward in, or deduced from, the message of President Monroe to Congress, December 2, 1823. "The American continents . . . are henceforth not to be considered as subjects for future colonization by any European powers." Although named after the president who delivered the message to Congress on December 2, 1823, the doctrine was penned by Secretary of State

John Quincy Adams. At his most forceful, Monroe declared, "And to the defense of our own [government], which has been achieved by the loss of so much blood and treasure, and matured by the wisdom of their most enlightened citizens, and under which we have enjoyed unexampled felicity, this whole nation is devoted."

Although not named by him, the Monroe Doctrine is the term and concept most closely associated with the fifth president who was, with George Washington, the only other president to have fought in the American Revolution. Thomas Jefferson immediately declared it the most important statement of policy since the nation became independent. But when was the doctrine so named? It appears to have taken awhile. The earliest citation in the *Oxford English Dictionary* is 1848, and that is not exact: "The President [Polk] had taken the opportunity of reiterating a doctrine which was said to be the doctrine of Mr. Monroe." It is not until 1850 that an example can be found for "Monroe Doctrine."[90]

Although Europe initially paid little attention to Monroe's words, the Monroe Doctrine became a tenet of American philosophy, permanently changing Europe's role in the Americas.

MOONDOGGLE. A taunt that was inspired by **President Kennedy** was *moondoggle* (*moon* + *boondoggle*), a portmanteau word coined to underscore the opinion that his 1961 plan to put Americans on the moon "before the decade is out" would prove to be an immense waste of money.[91]

MORAL EQUIVALENT OF WAR. Originally posited by William James in 1906 to mean a morally acceptable equivalent of the adventure and glory men thought they saw in war, and redefined seventy years later by **Jimmy Carter** to describe the energy challenge facing America[92]

MR. MADISON'S WAR. The War of 1812, so-called because on June 1, 1812, President **James Madison** asked Congress to declare war against Great Britain. He gave as his reasons the impressments—forced service—of Americans as seamen in the British Navy and interference with U.S. trade. He also charged that the British had stirred up Indian warfare in the

Northwest. Because Madison asked for the declaration of war, many Federalists blamed him for the conflict, calling it "Mr. Madison's war."

The city in Wisconsin and the avenue in Manhattan were both named for Madison in 1836, the year he died.

MUCKRAKER. Someone who searches out and makes public corruption by well-known officials, corporations, etc. The word quickly came to describe anyone who inquires into and publishes scandal and allegations of corruption among political and business leaders. The word was coined by **Theodore**

THE MUCK RAKE AND SOME OF THE MUCK.

Roosevelt in an April 15, 1906, speech condemning the activities of certain crusading journalists. Using imagery from John Bunyan's *Pilgrim's Progress*, he accused them of stirring up the muck of American society rather than raising their heads to see its heavenly crown of great advances in business and industry.

Roosevelt's comparison of irresponsible writers to the "Man with the Muck Rake" who could look no way but downward gave reformer Lincoln Steffens and his colleagues a descriptor they gleefully seized upon.

Later, Roosevelt admitted that those who adopted the title did the nation a great service in calling attention to needed reforms.* He said, "The men with the muckrakes are often in-

---

*This is from TR himself: "In Bunyan's *Pilgrim's Progress* you may recall the description of the Man with the Muck Rake, the man who could look no way but downward, with the muck rake in his hand; who was offered a celestial crown for his muck rake, but who would neither look up nor regard the crown he was offered, but continued to rake to himself the filth of the floor. In *Pilgrim's Progress* the Man with the Muck Rake is set forth as the example of him whose vision is fixed on carnal instead of spiritual things. Yet he also typifies the man who in this life consistently refuses to see aught that is lofty, and fixes his eyes with solemn intentness only on that which is vile and debasing. Now, it is very necessary that we should not flinch from seeing what is vile and debasing . . . There is filth on the floor, and it must be scraped up with the muck rake; and there are times and places where this service is the most needed of all the services that can be performed. But the man who never

dispensable to the well-being of society; but only if they know when to stop raking the muck, and look upward to the celestial crown above them, to the crown of worthy endeavor."

Although there is little question that Roosevelt popularized the word, it was being used in political circles in the nineteenth century. It appears in Maximilian Schele de Vere's *Americanisms*, published in 1872, as "a slang term . . . for persons who 'fish in troubled waters.'"

MULLIGAN. The golf custom employed by duffers to allow each player one "do over" of a drive per round of golf; by extension: a second chance. The term is of unknown origin (the *OED* says that it is named for someone named Mulligan) and saw limited use until being popularized by **Dwight Eisenhower**. On May 18, 1947, this practice first became newsworthy when the *Washington Post* reported that then "General Eisenhower got away from the first tee gracefully on his second shot, taking advantage of the rule of 'Mulligans' to smite one far down the middle after hooking his first shot into the trees." Ike used the term often, and a dozen newspaper stories about the president as golfer allude to his taking and giving mulligans on the first drive—although on one occasion in Pebble Beach in August 1956 he does not call it a mulligan but a "breakfast ball."

---

does anything else, who never thinks or speaks or writes, save of his feats with the muck rake, speedily becomes, not a help but one of the most potent forces for evil."

NANTUCKETER. A native or inhabitant of Nantucket. **Thomas Jefferson** put this demonym into play in 1788 in a report on U.S. commerce: "It will suffice to grant enough advantages . . . to forestall among the Nantucketers the desire to emigrate."[93]

"NATTERING NABOBS OF NEGATIVISM." Phrase coined by **William Safire** and uttered by Vice President **Spiro Agnew** to attack liberals, with whom he disagreed. Agnew elaborated alliteratively: "They have formed their own 4-H club—the hopeless, hysterical hypochondriacs of history." Agnew also described Democrats as "pusillanimous pussyfooters" and "vicars of vacillation," and accused them of offering voters "leap year lollipops"—programs appetizing to the eye but without much substance. All this prompted George McGovern to denounce Agnew's "foaming fusillades."

NATURE FAKERS. Term of derogation aimed at writers who create a counterfeit interpretation of nature and the behavior of animals in the wild. The term was coined in 1907 by **Theodore Roosevelt** amid a controversy that pitted the bona fide naturalists John Muir and John Burroughs against Ernest Thompson Seton, author of *Wild Animals I Have Known*, and the Reverend William Long, author of many children's books. Both Seton and Long saw the animal kingdom adhering to ethical codes of behavior based on an innate humanitarianism. Roosevelt considered this view of nature deranged and corrupting to the minds of the children, who were their major audience.

Long claimed to have observed muskrats, beavers, and bears setting broken bones and bandaging the stumps of chopped-off paws with pine pitch, spruce resin, or clay. He also claimed that animals had schools in which they taught their young to be insightful and prepared for a moral life in the wild. In his *Natural History of the Ten Commandments*, Seton argued that all creatures were required to obey biblical admonitions, and that promiscuous animals such as rabbits or polygamous animals such as elk were punished by God with diseases and infirmities unknown to other more virtuous members of the animal kingdom. In a relentlessly critical article on Nature Fakers, TR mocked these writers: "In one story, a wolf is portrayed as guiding home some lost children, in a spirit of thoughtful kindness . . . Again one of these story-book wolves, when starving, catches a red squirrel, which he takes round as a present to propitiate a bigger wolf. If any man seriously thinks a starving wolf would act in this manner, let him study hounds when feeding, even when they are not starving.[94]

NEOLOGIZE. To coin or use new words or phrases. Appropriately, **Thomas Jefferson**'s neologism for the process of

 creating neologisms. The word is first used in a letter to the grammarian John Waldo on August 16, 1813: "Necessity obliges us to neologize. And should the language of England continue stationary, we shall probably enlarge our employment of it [neologizing], until its ["American" English's] new character may separate it in name as well as in power, from the mother-tongue."

An 1820 letter from Jefferson to John Adams:

> I am a friend to neology. It is the only way to give to a language copiousness and euphony. Without it we should still be held to the vocabulary of Alfred [Alfred the Great, King of Wessex, 871–899] or of Ulphilas [a fourth-century Gothic bishop]; and held to their state of science also: for I am sure they had no words which could have conveyed the ideas of oxygen, cotyledons, zoophytes, magnetism, electricity, hyaline, and thousands of others expressing ideas not then existing, nor of possible communication in the state of their language. What a language has the French become since the date of their revolution, by the free introduction of new words! The most copious and eloquent in the living world; and equal to the Greek, had not that been regularly modifiable almost ad infinitum . . .

Dictionaries are but the depositories of words already legitimated by usage. Society is the workshop in which new ones are elaborated. When an individual uses a new word, if ill-formed it is rejected in society, if well-formed, adopted, and, after due time, laid up in the depository of dictionaries. And if, in this process of sound neologisation, our transatlantic brethren shall not choose to accompany us, we may furnish, after the Ionians, a second example of colonial dialect improving on its primitive.[95]

NEW DEAL. From the term as used in card playing, recast as the name for a new arrangement or system for obviating the disadvantages of an existing order and the official name for the program of massive economic and social reform initiated by **Franklin D. Roosevelt** to counteract the effects of the Great Depression. The original meaning of the term as the dealing of cards afresh at the start of a new game, rubber, or hand dates to 1746 in the sixth edition of Edmond Hoyle's *Short Treatise on the Game of Whist*, a rule book for the card game popular in the eighteenth and nineteenth centuries.

It reappears as a key term in FDR's July 2, 1932, acceptance speech at the Democratic National Convention: "I pledge you, I pledge myself, to a new deal for the American people. Let us all here assembled constitute ourselves prophets of a new order of competence and courage. This is more than a political campaign; it is a call to arms. Give me your help, not to win votes alone, but to win in this crusade to restore America to its own people."

The next day, a cartoon by Rollin Kirby in the *New York World-Telegram* showed a destitute farmer pausing to look in the sky where Roosevelt's aircraft flew overhead and on the wings were the words "New Deal." Until then, the campaign had done nothing to highlight the phrase.

"New Deal" stuck, and Roosevelt had a slogan to run on and, as president, a name for a vast expansion of the size and scope of the U.S. government to include caring for the nation's poor.

As metaphor derived from the dealing of playing cards, Jonathan Alter points out in *The Defining Moment: FDR's Hundred Days and the Triumph of Hope*, "The phrase 'new deal' had appeared as far back as Andrew Jackson's day, when Nicholas Biddle, the president of the Bank of the United States, called for a 'new bank and a New Deal.' It appeared in the novels of Mark Twain (*A Connecticut Yankee at King Arthur's Court*) and Henry James (*The Princess Casamassima*) and 'A New Deal for Everyone' was David Lloyd George's campaign slogan when he ran for prime minister of Great Britain in 1919."

The question remains: Who gave the words to FDR? Two of his speechwriters later claimed that they had reminted the phrase for him. Was it Judge Samuel Rosenman or the economist Stuart Chase, both of whom worked for Roosevelt? Chase's claim is simple enough. He wrote a June 29, 1932, cover story in the *New Republic* titled "A New Deal for America," during the week that Roosevelt gave his speech promising a new deal. It is "a dense piece of economic analysis arguing, in a sign of the times, that technological innovation was the cause of unemployment and should be stopped altogether."

In his book *Working with Roosevelt*, Rosenman gave his version. He was at the Executive Mansion in Albany on that July night when the nominating speeches were being made at the convention in Chicago. He described Roosevelt trying desperately to write a peroration to his acceptance speech, but there were so many telephone calls and other interruptions that the governor could not concentrate. Roosevelt read what he had written to the group, who pronounced it "terrible." Finally, at three in the morning, Rosenman decided to work on it, although at that time it looked as though Roosevelt would not win the nomination. Rosenman continued:

> I mention these details because the peroration I drafted had in it two words to which I gave little thought at the time, but which within a week became accepted as symbolic of the whole new philosophy and program of the Democratic candidate. Intended to epitomize the program of "bold, persistent experimentation" on behalf of the "forgotten man" the phrase was in the sentence, "I pledge you, I pledge myself, to a new deal for the American people."
>
> I had not the slightest idea that it would take hold the way it did, nor did the Governor when he read and revised what I had written. In fact, he attached no importance to the two monosyllables.
>
> Some have said that it was intended to be a combination of the square deal of President Theodore Roosevelt

and the new freedom of President Woodrow Wilson. There was no such intention when it was written or when it was delivered. It was intended to indicate that the old kind of political and economic thinking which had persisted in Washington during the last 12 years would come to an end if Roosevelt were elected.

Roosevelt himself had little to say on the matter until December 3, 1933, when Cyril Clemens, a distant cousin of Mark Twain, came to the White House to present him with a gold medal for oratory awarded him by the International Mark Twain Society. After the president said that Twain was his favorite author, Clemens asked FDR if he knew that the slogan of his administration was used by Twain in *A Connecticut Yankee in King Arthur's Court*.

"Yes, certainly I was aware of the fact," the president replied, "for it was there that I obtained the phrase. You recall the Yankee's saying that he was in a country where a right to say how the country should be governed was restricted to six persons in each thousand of its population. He found himself, so to speak, a stockholder in a corporation where nine hundred and ninety-four of the members furnished all the money and did all the work, and the other six elected themselves a permanent board of directors and took all the profits. And so he came to the logical and inescapable conclusion that what the nine hundred and ninety-four dupes needed was a new deal. I felt the same way about conditions in America as the Yankee did about those in ancient Britain.

"You have probably read various accounts of how I obtained the phrase, but they are all erroneous," Roosevelt continued.

"I freely acknowledge my debt to Mark Twain, whose entire works I hope to read over again after I return to Hyde Park."

Roosevelt then sent a letter to Clemens affirming in writing that the utterance of Hank in *Connecticut Yankee* was the true source inspiration for the New Deal.

A further attestation appeared in *The Saturday Review Literature* on December 16, 1933. "The President is quoted as stating in a recent interview that he took the phrase 'New Deal' from Mark Twain's Connecticut Yankee. Men take suggestions where they find their own beliefs expressed, and sometimes the source of the ideas is a clue to the borrower's thoughts. Twain said of the downtrodden subjects of King Arthur that what the 'nine hundred and ninety-four dupes needed was a new deal' and the editor connects this with Roosevelt's concern for the masses."[96]

NEW FEDERALISM. The term *new federalism* was coined by President **Richard Nixon**, who believed that the federal government had to be "more sensitive, receptive, and responsive to the views and wishes of state and local officials."

NEW FOUNDATION. An expression used by **Barack Obama** to encapsulate his ambitious program to pull the country out of the deep recession and to overhaul energy, education, and health care, similar to the effort of Franklin D. Roosevelt in the 1930s.

NEW FRONTIER. Program of social improvement advocated by **John F. Kennedy**, which demanded "new invention, innovation, imagination, decision." In his acceptance speech at the Democratic National Convention in 1960, Kennedy said, "The New Frontier of which I speak is not a set of promises— It is a set of challenges. It sums up not what I intend to offer the American people, but what I intend to ask of them. It appeals to their pride, not to their pocketbooks—it holds out the promise of more sacrifice instead of more security."[97]

NEW WORLD ORDER. State and time of assertive U.S. leadership and vision that would help to shape the twenty-first century. The term was coined by **George H. W. Bush** in a joint

session to Congress on September 11, 1990, during the buildup to the Gulf War (aka Operation Desert Storm, January 1991). Bush referred to the prospects of a new world order where the "rule of law supplants the rule of the jungle. A world in which nations recognize the shared responsibility for freedom and justice. A world where the strong respect the rights of the weak." The concept had precedence in the term "new order," which was used during the World War II years to describe "the system of regimentation imposed upon conquered countries by the Axis."[98]

NEW YORKER. A native or inhabitant of New York. In 1856, during the French and Indian War, the American soldiers from all the colonies were complaining to General **George Washington** that they were not paid enough to obtain bare necessities such as food and clothing. Washington, in turn, wrote to John Robinson, speaker of the House of Burgesses, the colonies' elected assembly and thus responsible for payments. "The Jerseys and New Yorkers, I do not know what it is they give [to their soldiers; that is, he doesn't know what they are paid]," he said. Perhaps this demonym was in use earlier, but Washington seems to have been among its earliest adopters, if not the man who coined it.

NIXON DOCTRINE. Policy declared by **Richard Nixon** in 1969 that the United States would supply arms but not military forces to its allies in Asia and elsewhere.

NORMALCY. A state, often more imagined than real, of a previous time when life and the affairs of the nation were in harmony. Following a world war and the aggressive progressive reforms of **Woodrow Wilson, Warren G. Harding** campaigned on the concept of "Steady America" and "Let's Be Done With Wiggle And Wobble." However, "A Return to Normalcy" and "Back to Normalcy" were his key campaign slogans. In his "return to normalcy" speech, Harding proclaimed, "The problems of maintained civilization are not to be solved by a transfer of responsibility from citizenship to government." If there was a key to Harding's 1920 campaign, it was in his call for what he termed "normalcy"—a cry for the state of the country before World War I: "America's present need is not heroics, but healing; not nostrums, but normalcy; not revolution, but restoration . . ."

The word preexisted in several areas, including mathematics, but Harding's use was created and defined as a political state. Although long mocked as a malapropism and an example of Harding's ineptitude with the language and his inability to use the "proper word," his nostalgic desire to return American to a more stable time probably helped get him elected in the largest landslide victory before or since.

In the days following the 9/11 attacks on the United States, **George W. Bush** used the word in the same sense that Harding did, this time alluding to the desire to return the nation to the pre-9/11 status quo.

OBAMACARE. A term of derogation for **Barack Obama's** Patient Protection and Affordable Care Act, which was proposed by the Democratic leadership and became law in March 2010. Elspeth Reeve, writing for the Atlantic Wire on October 26, 2011, traces the term back to the lobbyist Jeanne Schulte Scott, who argued in the trade journal *Healthcare Financial Management* in March 2007, that President Bush had "put all his eggs into his 'privatization' basket" in his recent State of the Union address; nevertheless, he made health-care the "issue du jour" for the 2008 presidential race. She added, "Health care is hot!" noting that the many would-be candidates for president in 2008 were falling over themselves offering their own proposals. She suggested that we would soon see "Giuliani-care" and "Obama-care" to go along with "McCain-care," "Edwards-care," and a totally revamped and remodeled "Hillary-care" from the 1990s.

Reeve said that Nancy Benac of the Associated Press appears to have reported the first derisive use of the word by a political candidate. On September 15, 2007, Benac wrote,

"Already, the GOP candidates are branding Democratic proposals a step on the road to socialized medicine while they offer incremental steps such as tax breaks to expand coverage and make it more affordable. 'Let me tell ya, if we don't do it, the Democrats will,' warns Republican Mitt Romney. 'And if the Democrats do it, it'll be socialized medicine. It will be government-managed care. It'll be what's known as Hillary-care or Barack Obama–care or whatever you want to call it.'"

By 2012, the word was almost ubiquitous, showing up in the writing of columnists including Kathleen Parker of the *Washington Post*, who defended its use by maintaining that it is widely used by journalists who are "strictly limited by word count." Mary M. Johnson of Frederick, Maryland, wrote in a letter that appeared in the July 21, 2012, *Post*: "Apparently, the term Obamacare is more convenient than 'The Affordable Care Act' and nothing more. Perhaps columnists, such as Parker, could begin using the terms: Lincolntalk, rather than 'The Gettysburg Address'; Jeffersonspeak, rather than 'The Declaration of Independence'; or, perhaps, Madison-rules, rather than 'The Constitution of the United States of America.' Surely these terms would be more convenient for columnists, and readers would soon catch on."[99]

OFF-DUTY. While not involved in one's regular responsibilities, especially in the context of the military. First encountered in **George Washington**'s *General Orders* of March 9, 1776: "The General earnestly expects every Officer and Soldier of this Army will show the utmost alertness, as well upon duty, as off duty, as by that means not only the utmost power but the utmost artifice of the enemy will be defeated."[100]

OFF-MESSAGE / ON-MESSAGE. Terms introduced by President-Elect **Bill Clinton** meaning to be in a position that is either in (on) or not in (off) accordance with a planned or intended message, especially so as to reinforce official party policy. *The Oxford English Dictionary* mentions the Clinton team in its examples for the first citation for these terms. "Although it [the Clinton transition team] harnessed masterfully the new prestige of the president-elect . . . , it has also endured a torrent of stories about such 'off message' matters as homosexuals in the military and the role of Hillary Clinton." And, "Since Super Tuesday, say the policy types, Clinton has been back 'on message,' although that doesn't erase the record."[101]

OK. The world's most universal of all terms of approval and assent—good, well, all correct, etc.—understood by speakers of virtually any language. Many explanations of its origin exist, but it seems to have originated as an abbreviation of *orl korrekt*, a jokey misspelling of "all correct," which was current in the United States in the 1830s and in print by 1839.[102]

But the term was popularized and underscored—although not coined, as many have suggested—from the nickname Old Kinderhook for **Martin Van Buren**, a native of Kinderhook, New York. During the election of 1840, Van Buren was supported by an O.K. Club, which campaigned vigorously for him.

OKEH. *OK* was spelled out as okeh by Woodrow Wilson in 1919 on the assumption that it represented Choctaw *okeh*—"it is so" (a theory that lacks historical documentation). According to H. L. Mencken in *American Language*, "Dr. Woodrow Wilson is said . . . to use *okeh* in endorsing government papers." This was replaced quickly by *okay* after the appearance of that form in 1929.

ONE HUNDRED PER CENT AMERICAN. A favorite phrase of **Theodore Roosevelt**, who may have coined it or certainly made it popular. It stands in contrast to the Rooseveltism *hyphenated American*.

ONE NATION. A nation that is not divided; a united indivisible people. **Thomas Jefferson** wrote to James Madison, "The politics of Europe render it indispensably necessary that with respect to everything external we be one nation only, firmly hooped together."[103]

ONE-PAGER. A cheat sheet. As defined by Bill Timmons, former aide to presidents Nixon and Ford, "a piece of paper containing all of the information on an issue, from geologic formations at Anwar in Alaska to complex tax proposals totally incomprehensible in their completed form. It stemmed from a time when Henry Kissinger gave Richard Nixon two pages, he told him, 'Henry, I want this on one page.' Kissinger turned to a secretary and said, 'Retype this on one page.'"

"THE ONLY THING WE HAVE TO FEAR IS FEAR ITSELF." With this phrase from his first inaugural address on

 March 4, 1933, **Franklin D. Roosevelt** encouraged Americans to look with confidence to the future, never mind the Great Depression or a world inching toward global conflict. Robert E. Sherwood wrote, "Mr. Roosevelt worked very hard on all of his important speeches. The preparation of the speech would often take a week or more. By the time it was finished every sentence would be stamped by Roosevelt with his own character. When he delivered the speech it became a living thing."

OTTOMAN. A low upholstered footstool without a back or arms, typically serving also as a box, with the seat hinged to form a lid. A 1789 memorandum from **Thomas Jefferson** notes that he "p[ai]d. for an Ottomane of velours d'Utrecht." Jefferson was not the coiner of this term but rather the one who appears to have brought it to English. Ottomans were in France, as was Jefferson, where the spelling was *ottomane*.[104]

"OUR LONG NATIONAL NIGHTMARE." Characterization of the Watergate era uttered by **Gerald Ford,** on assuming the presidency after the 1974 resignation of Richard Nixon, when he told the nation, "My fellow Americans, our long national nightmare is over." The memorable phrase, actually coined by **Robert T. Hartmann,** counselor to the president, almost failed to survive. In an ABC News program in 1985 that examined major events of the previous three decades, Ford spoke of the turmoil of the Watergate scandal, which

had brought down his prede-
cessor. He recalled that on the
morning of August 9, 1974,
he bade farewell just before
Nixon boarded a helicopter
on the White House grounds.
"Words weren't very easy to
come by," he said. Minutes
later, Ford was looking at the
proposed text of the nationally
televised speech he was to give

from the East Room of the White House after taking the oath
of office at noon. One line troubled him, the one about the
"national nightmare." "I thought that was a little harsh," he
recalled, "and I said, 'Bob, I think we ought to strike that.'"
Hartmann states in *Palace Politics: An Insider's Account of the
Ford Years* that he had immediately threatened to resign if the
phrase was excised.[105]

OVERDRAUGHT. When more money is drawn from an account than the account holds. The word debuts in an 1812
letter from **Thomas Jefferson** to the mercantile firm of Gibson
& Jefferson: "Whether I shall have flour in your hands . . . [in
time] to cover the overdraughts will depend on the state of the
two rivers [on which the mills are located]."[106]

OWNERSHIP SOCIETY. **George W. Bush**'s term for his
effort to introduce private accounts to Social Security and expand the use of defined contribution programs for retirement
and health savings.

PACK RAT. Any of several rodents of North and Central America, of the genus *Neotoma* and related genera of the family Muridae, noted for collecting sticks and other materials and accumulating them within their nests. Also called *trade-rat* and *woodrat*, the name *pack rat* was bestowed upon these creatures by **Theodore Roosevelt** in 1885 when he wrote in his diary, "These rats were christened pack rats, on account of their curious and inveterate habit of dragging off to their holes every object they can possibly move. From the hole of one, underneath the wall of a hut, I saw taken a small revolver, a hunting-knife, two books, a fork, a small bag, and a tin cup."[107] As early as 1912 the name was reapplied to a person who hoards things, as in, "He comes from a family of pack rats—keepers of everything that comes into their house."

PARLOR PACIFIST. A term created by **Theodore Roosevelt** in 1917 to describe a person who is a pacifist in dinner table conversations but never does anything more with his convictions than express them to others. There were other denizens of the parlor in his vocabulary, including the *parlor Bolshevist* given to radical ranting without subsequent action. *Parlor* became a modifier with a sting.

Later, someone other than TR came up with *parlor Pink* to cover those with mildly radical opinions who were almost Red— also known as *pinkos*. In Roosevelt's time and well into the twentieth century, larger houses contained a parlor, a room set aside to entertain visitors. *Parlor* comes from the French *parler*, which means "to talk."

PAROLED. Of a prisoner: put or released on parole. **George Washington** in a letter of October 13, 1782, to Major General Henry Knox, who was assigned to negotiate prisoner exchanges with the British: "I cannot consent to send them [prisoners of war] to New York, as with an old Balance and those who have gone in with paroled officers, the enemy already owe us 900 Men."[108]

PEACE WITH HONOR. The aim of U.S. peace negotiations with North Vietnam, as coined by **Lyndon Johnson**. After Richard Nixon became president in 1968, his policy toward Vietnam was an "honorable peace." The United States could not "win" the war, but neither was it prepared to "lose" it—or to lose face.

PEDICURE. French for care of the feet, toes, and toenails, and by extension the act of caring for the feet. **Thomas Jefferson** wrote in his personal memoranda for December 29, 1784: "P[ai]d La Forest pedicure 12f."[109]

PERSONAL SHOPPER. It appears that this term was coined by **Jacqueline Kennedy** in a November 14, 1960, letter to her favorite hat saleswoman at Bergdorf Goodman, an exclusive New York City department store. The term was minted as Kennedy was preparing for Inauguration Day and wrote to Marita O'Connor at the store's custom hat department for help in selecting other accessories. "Can I sort of use you as my personal shopper there?" she wrote to O'Connor in a letter that came to light when thirteen letters from Kennedy to O'Connor were auctioned off at Sotheby's in 1998 after the saleswoman's death.[110]

PHOTO OPPORTUNITY. Term that came from the administration of **Richard Nixon** for a scripted moment for the cameras. According to William Safire, one day Nixon said to an aide, Bruce Whelihan, "Get 'em [the White House press corps] in here for a picture." Whelihan announced to the press room, "There will be a photo opportunity in the Oval Office."[111]

POLICE STATE METHODS. A state regulated by means of national police is a police state, a term first recorded in 1865 with reference to Austria and applied often to Nazi Germany. In October 1947, **Harry Truman** remarked that government compulsions—whatever the emergency that might have required them—are the methods of police states and not true republics or democracies, an idea that was most upsetting to his political advisers. Truman was alluding to the price, wage, and rent controls as well as rationing imposed on the nation during World War II. The comment led Arthur Krock of the *New York Times* to term Truman a Jeffersonian Democrat rather than a New Dealer and underscored the point that Truman may have been one of the nation's most uninhibited presidents.[112]

POLITICS IS ADJOURNED. **Woodrow Wilson**'s creation and widely used by government officials and politicians after the United States declared war on Germany on April 6, 1917. It was intended to unite the people of all political parties behind the president and the army in training men, getting men and ammunition to Europe, and securing the cooperation of farmers, merchants, manufacturers, educators, and all other groups of Americans in preparing for and successfully conducting the war so as to defeat German militarism.[113]

POTOMAC FEVER. Common affliction causing people to become obsessed with attaining and maintaining power in Washington, D.C. "It was **Woodrow Wilson** who coined the phrase," Harry Truman explained in his oral biography, *Plain Speaking.* Truman continued:

> He said that some people came to Washington and grew with their jobs, but he said a lot of other people came, and all they did was swell up. Those that swell up are the ones that have Potomac Fever. They're the people who forget who they are and who sent them there.
> *Did you ever feel you were in any danger of doing that?*
> No, no. I always came back to Independence every

chance I got because the people in Independence, the people in Missouri had been responsible for sending me to Washington. And that's why when I ended up at the White House, after I had finished the job, I came back here. This is where I belong.[114]

Despite Truman's attribution to Wilson, it was Truman who put the term on the lexical map. From the September 1946 issue of *American Notes and Queries*: "Potomac fever—Il-

lusion of power and statesmanship fostered by a comfortable, padded existence in Washington, D.C.; coined by President Truman and applied by him to Senator Burton K. Wheeler."

The term gained popularity in 1951 when the author Fletcher Knebel began a long-running nationally syndicated column called "Potomac Fever." In 1991, Representative Patricia Schroeder (D-CO) noted George H. W. Bush's twenty-fifth year in Washington and said, "When it comes to Potomac Fever, George Bush is a carrier." Schroeder said at the time that Bush, Vice President Dan Quayle, and the cabinet secretaries had together piled up 230 years in Washington. "There are a number of things wrong with Washington," Dwight Eisenhower said. "One of them is that everyone has been too long away from home."

POTUS. Acronym for President Of The United States, who is often in the company of FLOTUS, the First Lady Of The

United States. The two are usually in CONUS (the CONtinental United States), except when they're OCONUS (Outside the CONtinental United States). According to the *Wall
Street Journal*, this acronym was a favorite of Lyndon Johnson's
but displeased Richard Nixon, who preferred to be called "the
president" and did away with POTUS. It came back during
the Kennedy administration and has been used by all the ad-
ministrations since then. The term actually dates back to 1879
and the administration of **Rutherford B. Hayes**. It was part of
a code copyrighted by Walter P. Phillips, at the time the Washington bureau chief for the Associated Press, which was described as "a thoroughly tested method of shorthand arranged
for telegraphic purposes and contemplating the rapid trans-
mission of press reports; also intended to be used as an easily
acquired method for general and court reporting." Phillips also
used SCOTUS for Supreme Court Of The United States.[115]

PREBUTTAL. A statement made in anticipation of a criticism or question; a preemptive rebuttal. The word was coined
in 1986 by Vice President **Al Gore**, but it didn't make its debut in the press until May 26, 1996, in the *Washington Post*:
"President Clinton's White House and campaign team have
been drawing favorable reviews for their rapid response operation and penchant for picking off issues before Senate Majority
Leader Robert J. Dole . . . even gets his TelePrompTer warmed
up. Vice President Gore calls it 'prebuttal.'"

PRESS ROOM. **Teddy Roosevelt** set up the first modern
press room in the White House. The term existed prior to this
for other occasions, but he is the one who gave its modern

context. As Bruce L. Felknor says of TR in *Political Mischief: Smear, Sabotage, and Reform in U.S. Elections*, "He was a public relations natural before the term was coined. His youth, vitality, and candor were admired and enjoyed by reporters, and this affection outlasted his presidential tenure." Jimmy Carter, a president who was hardly a PR natural, often dropped by the White House press room, "guaranteeing himself a few precious seconds of 'face time' on the evening TV news."[116]

PRESSING THE FLESH. This term for shaking hands was originally *jive talk* dating back to the 1930s and 1940s and hip slang of Cab Calloway and others, but it became political slang during **Lyndon Johnson**'s 1960 campaign as the Democratic vice presidential candidate. He is recorded as telling a crowd: "You make us feel so wonderful to come out here and look us in the eye and give us a chance to press the flesh with you."

"A PUBLIC OFFICE IS A PUBLIC TRUST." A campaign slogan of **Grover Cleveland**, who was a stern advocate and adherent of honest public service. The phrase was coined by **William C. Hudson**, a publicity man working for Cleveland who had taken Cleveland's thoughts on public service and turned them into a slogan—in this sense these are Cleveland's words. As Rexford Tugwell maintains in his biography of Cleveland, the president's major virtue was honesty—"a man of immovable integrity in a time of sleazy morality." He adds, "It would be hard for later generations to conceive that PUBLIC OFFICE IS A PUBLIC TRUST could distinguish one man from whole generations of contemporaries; but it was so."[117]

PUSSYFOOTER. Originally, a person who moves quietly or stealthily in the manner of a cat; later, someone who behaves in a sly, furtive, or underhanded way, or who acts evasively or in an excessively cautious or hesitant manner.

The first use of the word is credited to **Teddy Roosevelt** in 1911, when he said, "They ask that . . . this Senate adjourn and say to this board of managers and their counsel and their corps of detectives and their pussy-footers, go out over the state again and gather up a few cases and come back here." TR certainly used the term early and often, and he appears to be the author of *pussyfooter*—as well as the next logical variation, *pussy-footism*: "Roosevelt declares against pussy-footism, by which, we take it, he is in favor of a fight in the open."

Another influence on Roosevelt was almost certainly the nickname for William E. "Pussyfoot" Johnson (1862–1945), a staunch prohibitionist and respected chief law enforcement officer for the U.S. Indian Service. He implemented effective "catlike policies in pursuing lawbreakers in the Indian Territory," as he himself explained in *Who's Who in America*, obtaining some forty-four hundred convictions during his tenure (1908–1911).

As Albert Marckwardt points out in *American English*: "Johnson was also active in the Anti-Saloon League and frequently lectured on temperance. Not only was he instrumental in the passage of Prohibition in 1919, he took the 'cause' to London, where it was not always met with enthusiasm. In fact at Essex Hall an angry lush in the crowd he was lecturing to threw a stone and blinded him in one eye."[118]

QUIXOTIC. **John Adams,** an avid reader, used Cervantes's hero Don Quixote as an adjective characterizing unrealistic schemes—which were hardly uncommon during the early days of the Republic. He wrote to Senator James Lloyd of Massachusetts in 1815, "I considered Miranda as a vagrant, a vagabond, a Quixotic adventurer." (He was referring to General Francisco de Miranda, a Venezuelan revolutionary with a plan to liberate and unify all of Spanish America.) Although Adams is listed as the first citation in the *Dictionary of American English* and in early editions of the *Oxford English Dictionary*, recent research has revealed earlier users of the word, so Adams must be listed as a popularizer of this Americanism with roots in Spanish literature.[119]

RACIAL DISCRIMINATION. The word *discrimination* dates back to the seventeenth century, but the making of distinctions prejudicial to people of a different race or color from oneself comes from a speech given by **Andrew Johnson** on March 27, 1866. Johnson was explaining his veto of the Civil Rights Act. He complained that the bill gave rights to Congress that had previously been reserved to the states: "Thus a perfect equality of the white and colored races is attempted to be fixed by Federal law in every State of the Union over the vast field of State jurisdiction covered by these enumerated rights. In no one of these can any State ever exercise any power of discrimination between the different races."[120] Johnson said he did not object to equality per se, but he envisioned what today he might have called a slippery slope, where Congress could enact laws before the states were ready for them. On April 9, 1866, the act was passed over his veto.

REAGAN DOCTRINE. Name given to the idea that the United States should use any means possible to topple left-wing regimes it does not like, such as the case of the covert war on Nicaragua. The eponymously named doctrine was created by **Ronald Reagan**'s critics. "Look around you and you can see that the policy has had significant results," wrote Anthony Lewis in the *New York Times* on April 24, 1987. "It has corrupted our own institutions: intelligence, the military, the White House. It has spread disdain for democracy and for law."

This was of course not the first (or last) policy to be elevated to a "doctrine"—the Monroe and Truman doctrines were familiar. So was the Carter Doctrine, the principles of which were included in the president's State of the Union address in 1980: The United States would use military force if necessary to protect its national interests in the Persian Gulf. In addition there is the 2001 so-called Bush Doctrine (which received that moniker from Charles Krauthammer in the *Washington Post*), with its policy of preventive war against regimes that posed a potential or perceived—not necessarily immediate—threat to the United States.*

REAGANISM. Eponym first recorded in 1966 in reference to the policies of **Ronald Reagan**, governor of California 1967–1975; U.S. president 1981–1989.

REAGANOMICS. Name for the economic policies of **Ronald Reagan**, from *Reagan + economics*, first used in 1981. The president advocated cutting programs and taxes, increasing defense spending, reducing government regulation, and encouraging

---

*Not to mention the Nixon Doctrine, Clinton Doctrine, Obama Doctrine, Powell Doctrine, [Caspar] Weinberger Doctrine, [Paul] Wolfowitz Doctrine . . .

private investment by the wealthy so that the benefits would trickle down through the economy. The most loyal subscribers to this theory were dubbed "Reaganauts."

RECONNOITER. From the French, an adoption from the same stem as *reconnaissance*, used by **George Washington**. To Brigadier-General David Waterbury in 1781: "The ap-

proach from the inner Point (mentioned in the Reconnoitre from the Jersey shore) is secured by a ledge of Rocks, which would conceal a party from observation, till it got within about one hundred yards of the fort," and to Major-General Charles C. Pinckney in 1799: "Your report . . . and . . . your reconnoi-tre of the seaboard to St. Mary's, and visit to the posts on the Indian frontier . . . will be made to the Department of War."[121]

REENLIST. To sign up for a tour of duty again; especially to enlist in the armed forces again. From **George Washington**'s General Orders in 1775: "Daniel Carmiele [of the military force of Philadelphia] . . . tried for 'Disobedience of orders, for reinlisting and taking advance Money twice over, and for Drunkenness.'"[122]

REHIRE. To employ again. **George Washington** wrote to his niece, Fanny, advising her on how to run the plantation left to her by her late husband: ". . . Nor ought there to be any transfer of the lease, or re-hire of the Negros without your consent first had & obtained in writing."[123]

RESIGNATE. To resonate. Coined in this sense by **George W. Bush** ("This issue doesn't seem to resignate with the people." Portland, Oregon, October 31, 2000). Although often cited as a prime Bush malaprop, the word appears in the *Oxford English Dictionary*, meaning "to resign," first showing up in 1531–1532. The *OED*, does, however, note that the word's use is "rare."

"A RISING TIDE LIFTS ALL BOATS." Widely attributed to **John F. Kennedy** from his remarks in Heber Springs, Arkansas, at the Dedication of Greers Ferry Dam on October 3, 1963: "These projects produce wealth, they bring industry, they bring jobs, and the wealth they bring brings wealth to other sections of the United States. This State had about 200,000 cars in 1929. It has a million cars now. They weren't built in this State. They were built in Detroit. As this State's income rises, so does the income of Michigan. As the income of Michigan rises, so does the income of the United States. A rising tide lifts all the boats and as Arkansas becomes more prosperous so does the United States and as this section declines so does the United States. So I regard this as an investment by the people of the United States in the United States."

President Kennedy used the phrase again in an address at Paulskirche in Frankfurt, West Germany, June 25, 1963 (one day before his famous "Ich bin ein Berliner" speech): "As they say on my own Cape Cod, a rising tide lifts all the boats. And a partnership, by definition, serves both partners, without domination or unfair advantage. Together we have been partners in adversity—let us also be partners in prosperity."

This is a clear example of a phrase that was made popular by a president rather than one he created. In his memoir *Counselor: A Life at the Edge of History*, Kennedy's speechwriter Ted Sorensen revealed that the phrase was neither his nor the president's. During his first year working for Kennedy, when Kennedy was still a senator from Massachusetts, Sorensen was trying to address economic problems in New England and happened upon the phrase. He noticed that "the regional chamber of commerce, the New England Council, had a thoughtful slogan: 'A rising tide lifts all the boats.'" From then on, JFK would borrow the slogan often.[124]

ROORBACK. A false, dirty, or slanderous story used for political advantage, usually about a candidate seeking political office. The term is an eponym for the Baron von Roorback, the invented author of an imaginary book from which a passage was quoted in an attempt to defame Tennessee governor **James Polk** during his 1844 presidential campaign against Henry Clay. Polk, who was in fact a major slaveholder, was further vilified by the "Roorback report," which appeared shortly before Election Day. The *Ithaca* (New York) *Chronicle* published an excerpt from Baron Roorback's journal *A Tour Through the Western and Southern States*. The baron told of watching the purchase of forty-three slaves by Polk, "the present Speaker of the House of Representatives, the mark of the branding iron and the initials of his name on their shoulders, distinguishing them." Other newspapers that shared the *Chronicle*'s Whig leanings just had time to copy its report before the election. Polk won, but the lie had spread widely enough to sully his reputation.

The roorback eponym was refined over time and defined in 1940 in the *Chicago Tribune* as a "false report about some alleged misdeed in a candidate's past, often based on forged evidence, circulated in the final days of a campaign. It is timed for climactic effect when the candidate will not be able to expose the fraud before the voters go to the polls."[125]

ROUGH RIDER. Originally a Western cowboy—as in Buffalo Bill's Wild West and Congress of Rough Riders—but later applied by **Theodore Roosevelt** to his regiment in the Spanish-American War. Writing in the *Century Magazine* in 1888, Roosevelt said, "The rough-rider of the plains, the hero of rope and revolver, is first cousin to the backwoodsman of the Southern Alleghanies, the man of the ax and the rifle; he is only a unique offshoot of the frontier stock of the South-west."[126]

"Rough Riders" was the name given to the First U.S. Volunteer Cavalry under the leadership of Roosevelt. The original plan for this unit called for filling it with men from the Indian Territory, New Mexico, Arizona, and Oklahoma. Once Roosevelt joined the group, its volunteers included Ivy League athletes and glee club singers. Roosevelt came home from Cuba with the Rough Riders after their charge up San Juan Hill as a hero, to be elected governor of New York State. He took pride in riding rough over politicians and vested interests that stood in his way.

SACRED COW. Allusion to an object of Hindu veneration, from 1891; figurative sense of something or someone who is beyond criticism first recorded 1910. The term became controversial during World War II when it was revealed that it was the code name for the C-54 aircraft used to take **Franklin D. Roosevelt** to the Yalta Conference. This code name became public when Roosevelt learned it, and it was used during the rest of his administration and by the Truman administration. A steady stream of letters to the White House complained that calling an aircraft by this name was "sacrilegious." By October 1946, the name was deemed a political embarrassment for Truman as the letters of protest were now constant and it became a matter for discussion in an October 26 press conference. The *New York Times* remarked that "the only way the Administration can escape the embarrassment, so well fixed has the nickname become, is by obtaining a new plane."[127]

SANCTION. To give approval, to make valid or binding (also the opposite: to punish for breaking a law). One of **Thomas**

Jefferson's suggested additions to Virginia's penal code sent to George Wythe, a lawyer, judge, and a mentor of Jefferson, on November 1, 1778. He explained his thinking: "I have aimed at accuracy, brevity, and simplicity; preserving, however, the very words of the established law, wherever their meaning had been sanctioned by judicial decisions, or rendered technical by usage."[128]

SECRETARY OF SEMANTICS. Name for an imaginary cabinet position created by **Harry Truman** in December 1947: "I have appointed a Secretary of Semantics—a most important post. He is to furnish me with forty to fifty dollar words. Tell me how to say yes and no in the same sentence without a contradiction. He is to tell me the combination of words that will put me against inflation in San Francisco and for it in New York. He is to show me how to keep silent—and say everything. You can very well see how he can save me an immense amount of worry."

SHAG. A copulatory verb which, according to the *Oxford English Dictionary*, first appeared in a memorandum of **Thomas Jefferson** in 1770. The context in which Jefferson used the term is in keeping with the vulgarity in question: "He had shagged his mother and begotten himself on her body." The first time the word shows up in a dictionary of slang is not until 1788.[129]

SHANGRI-LA. A fictional Himalayan Utopia described in James Hilton's 1933 novel *Lost Horizon*; henceforth anyplace, real or imagined, that approaches perfection. **Franklin D.**

Roosevelt was much enamored of the book and named the presidential retreat Shangri-La (now known as Camp David) in 1942. After the raid on Tokyo on April 18, 1942, led by Jimmy Doolittle, Roosevelt was asked where the bombers came from. He replied, "Shangri-La." Later in the war, the navy would launch an *Essex*-class aircraft carrier named the USS *Shangri-La* (CV-38) as a result of this reference.

SHOVEL-READY. Describing a building or project capable of being initiated immediately. The term was made famous by President-Elect **Barack Obama**, alluding to things that would begin as soon funding was approved by Congress.

SILENT CAL. This nickname was bestowed upon **Calvin Coolidge** because of his taciturn nature and also because of such statements as, "I have noticed that nothing I never said ever did me any harm." He was so famous for saying so little that a White House dinner guest made a bet that she could get him to say more than two words. When she told the president of her wager, he answered laconically, "You lose."

In 1920, Coolidge, preparing to run for the Republican nomination, entertained a reporter from the *New York Times* at his home in Northampton, Massachusetts, who reported, "There is a little framed legend over the cheerful open fireplace in the parlor of his home which may or may not have a bearing on his character. It reads:

A wise old owl lived in an oak:
The more he saw the less he spoke:

The less he spoke the more he heard
Why can't we be like that old bird?"[130]

SILENT MAJORITY. Originally those who supported President Nixon's policies but who were not politically vocal or active and considered by him to constitute a majority. Thence, any group of people who are not outspoken and who are considered a majority. William Safire defined it in his *Political Dictionary* as "the remarkable legion of the unremarked." **Richard Nixon** coined the term in this context in his November 3, 1969, speech on the Vietnam War to describe Americans who were not part of the loud, angry debate about ending the war but were "simply hoping that the nation could achieve a just and honorable peace." Nixon concluded, "It is time for the great silent majority of Americans to stand up and be counted." "*Silent Majority* is brilliant political language," William Safire was quoted in Israel Shenker's *Harmless Drudges*. "Oddly, the president was not trying to make a phrase. He didn't capitalize silent majority in the course of the speech, nor did he expect it to be picked out as a key line."[131] *

SLOGANEER. A person who invents and uses slogans to sell products as well as politicians. On August 20, 1932, the Democratic nominee for president, **Franklin Roosevelt**, gave a campaign speech in Columbus, Ohio, in which he said (in ref-

---

*Silent majority was used in the nineteenth century to refer to the dead. In 1902, Supreme Court Justice John Marshall Harlan said in a speech that the "great captains of both sides of our Civil War have long ago passed over to the silent majority, leaving the memory of their splendid courage."

erence to the Republican program of "Buy more! Owe more! Spend more!"), "It was the heyday of promoters, sloganeers, mushroom millionaires, opportunists, adventurers of all kinds." (A mushroom millionaire is an upstart, that is, someone who suddenly and recently struck it rich.) This gave rise to reports that Roosevelt had invented a new word, including an article the October 1932 issue of *Word Study*, a publication of the G. & C. Merriam Company. But even dictionary makers can be wrong. The December issue of *Word Study* contained a correction. The word had appeared as early as the April 29, 1922, issue of the *Saturday Evening Post* in a short story titled "Once a Sloganeer" by Richard Connell (about his years in advertising), who gets credit for the noun that Roosevelt made popular. However, FDR's *sloganeer* had more of a bite to it, implying someone who sells something that people do not actually need or want or afford, and in that context can be considered neologistic.[132]

SMOKE-FILLED ROOM. Another term drifting out from the **Warren G. Harding** campaign was *smoke-filled room*, a place where secret political deal making took place. In earlier eras, political deals were made behind closed doors where dense cigar smoke filled the air. The original smoke-filled room was located in Chicago's Blackstone hotel, where, according to an enduring legend, a small group of powerful U.S. senators gathered to arrange the nomination of Harding as Republican candidate for president in 1920. When the Associated Press reported that Harding had been chosen "in a smoke-filled room," the phrase entered the American political lexicon. Ever since, it has meant a place behind the scenes where cigar-smoking party bosses intrigue to choose candidates.[133]

SNOLLYGOSTER (also *snallygaster*). According to H. L. Mencken, "a snollygaster, apparently confined to the South, was a political jobseeker who wants office, regardless of party, platform or principles, and who, whenever he wins, gets thereby sheer force of monumental talknophical assumacy." Someone, especially a politician, who is guided by personal advantage rather than by consistent, respectable principles. A shrewd or unprincipled person, an unprincipled political job seeker.

In a 1952 speech, **Harry Truman** defined the word erroneously as a "man born out of wedlock." He was corrected by newspaper reporters, who relied on Mencken for all things linguistic. In *The American Language*, Mencken referred to the years 1812 to 1861 as a time of "uncouth neologisms" and included this among such words.

William Safire used Truman as an exemplar in 1980: "That's a power a President has—to bring back old words, as Harry Truman did with *snollygoster*—a linguistic power that Reagan will soon discover."

According to the *OED*, it began life as two German words: *schnelle geister*, meaning "quick spirits." A *schnelle geister* was a scary, ghostly apparition, and a snollygoster was a fabulous reptilian bird in Maryland, designed to scare the former slaves into not voting.[134]

SNOWMAGEDDON. This play on the word *Armageddon* was uttered by **Barack Obama** at a meeting of the Democratic National Committee at the Capital Hilton in Washington on the morning of February 6, 2010, as the city was experiencing a ferocious blizzard. "Oh, it is good to see you," he said in response to welcoming applause. "Good to be among friends so committed to the future of this party and this country that they're willing to brave a blizzard. *Snowmageddon* here in D.C." By the time the snow stopped, more than two feet had fallen on the White House, and the neologism was making its way around the English-speaking world.* Forecasters also popularized *snowpocalypse*. Both words were picked up by the Global Language Monitor as meeting their criteria for accepted new words, based on the number of English usages. (Other new coinages, such as *snownami*, have not yet won acceptance.)

Obama did not in fact create the word; he made it popular. The earliest use in a major newspaper was in a headline in the December 19, 2008, issue of the *Globe and Mail* (Toronto): "Ontario, Quebec brace for 'snowmageddon.'" As the blizzard was first being forecast, the *Washington Post* ran an online poll asking for reader feedback on the impending event and contained the words *Snowmageddon* and *Snowpocalypse* during the following days leading up to Obama's use of the word.

SOCIAL SECURITY. A state-run system providing financial support for people who are unemployed, sick, retired, or otherwise in need. The earliest example appears, according to the *Oxford English Dictionary*, in the construction *social security apparatus*

---

*Washington's heaviest snow on record was twenty-eight inches in January 1922. The biggest snowfall for the Washington-Baltimore area is believed to have been in 1772, before official records were kept, when as much as three feet fell, which both George Washington and Thomas Jefferson wrote about in their diaries.

in a 1908 letter written by **Winston Churchill**: "If we were able to underpin the whole existing social security apparatus with a foundation of comparatively low-grade state safeguards, we should in the result obtain something that would combine the greatest merits both of the English & the German systems."[135] Churchill was responsible for other terms that had clear impact on America, including *fly-in* (the act of delivering troops, goods, etc., by air to a specified place), *undefendable, underemployed, nippiness, well-entrenched,* and *seaplane.*

SOCKDOLAGER. Something outstanding or exceptional; something that settles a matter, a decisive blow or answer (first used in 1930 with the latter meaning). This is not a word made famous by a president but one that became infamous because of the context in which it appeared. On April 14, 1865, a variation was one of the last words President **Abraham Lincoln** heard during the performance of Tom Taylor's *Our American Cousin.* Taylor, who was British, had reputedly put the very American word into the play to Americanize its hero. According to Harry Hawk, the actor who was delivering the line in question in Act 3, scene 2, John Wilkes Booth, who was well acquainted with the play, waited for the line and the laughter that would follow it to act.

"Well, I guess I know enough to turn you inside out, old gal—you sockdologizing old man-trap."

As the audience laughed, Booth fired the fatal shot.[136]

"SPEAK SOFTLY AND CARRY A BIG STICK; YOU WILL GO FAR." During **Theodore Roosevelt**'s term as governor of New York State, he fought with the party bosses, particularly

Boss Tom Platt, regarding a political appointment. Roosevelt held out, although the boss threatened to "ruin" him. In the end, the boss gave in. According to Nathan Miller in *Theodore Roosevelt: A Life*, "Looking back upon his handling of the incident, Roosevelt thought he 'never saw a bluff carried more resolutely through to the final limit.' And writing to a friend a few days later, he observed: 'I have always been fond of the West African proverb: "Speak softly and carry a big stick; you will go far."'"

The proverb and the policy followed him throughout his career, including his policies abroad during his presidency. "There is a homely adage which runs, 'Speak softly and carry a big stick; you will go far.' If the American nation will speak softly and yet build and keep at a pitch of the highest training a thoroughly efficient navy, the Monroe Doctrine will go far."[137]

SPEC. A commercial venture; short for *speculation*. Created by **John Adams,** who first used it on April 1, 1794, in discussing trade issues: "Speculation mingles itself in every political operation, and many merchants have made a noble *spec.* of the embargo [on all ships, foreign or American, in the port of Philadelphia] by raising their prices."[138]

SPIN DOCTOR. A term that came out of the **Ronald Reagan** administration. Spin is endemic during election campaigns, as each side tries to push its own interpretation of events and discredit the other side's. According to the *Economist*, the term was coined in Reagan's first term and became important after the first 1984 Reagan-Mondale presidential debate in Louisville. By the time of the 1988 Bush-Dukakis debate at Wake Forest University, there were so many "spinners" working for each candidate that the *Washington Post* declared a postdebate state of "spinlock."

SPOILS SYSTEM. The practice of a successful political party removing appointed officials from the previous administration and replacing them with members of their own party. After entering the White House in 1829 and removing and replacing a group of John Quincy Adams's office holders, **Andrew Jackson** wrote in his diary, "Now, every man who has been in office a few years, believes he has a life estate in it, a vested right, and if it has been held twenty years or upwards, not only a vested right, but that it ought to descend to his children, and if no children then to the next of kin. This is not the principles of our government. It is rotation in office that will perpetuate our liberty."

The word *spoils*, meaning plunder taken from an enemy, had been around since the fourteenth century. But it wasn't until 1832, that Senator William L. Marcy, in his remarks to the Senate, said, "To the victor belong the spoils of the enemy," in effect declaring it as policy. And from this came the term *spoils system*, which was everlastingly attached to Jackson's ascendancy to office and marked the beginning of a system of party patronage that continues to this day.[139]

SPUTNIK MOMENT. A point where people realize that they are threatened or challenged and have to redouble their efforts to catch up. It dates from 1957, when the Soviet Union

 launched the first satellite, the Sputnik 1, and beat the United States into space. "A Sputnik moment is a trigger mechanism, an event that makes people collectively say that they need to do something, and this sets a course in another direction," said Roger Launius, senior curator of the National Air and Space Museum's Division of Space History at the Smithsonian Institution.

The term was coined and proclaimed by **Barack Obama** in his 2011 State of the Union address: "This is our generation's Sputnik moment . . . We need to reach a level of research and development we haven't seen since the height of the Space Race . . . We'll invest in biomedical research, information technology, and especially clean energy technology." In the same section of the speech, he likened this funding effort to the Apollo project, which later put a man on the moon.

SQUARE DEAL. (1) In card games, an honest, fair dealing or distribution of cards, a term that, according to Mathews's *Dictionary of Americanisms*, first appeared in Mark Twain's *Life on the Mississippi*. (2) An Americanism for a fair and honest arrangement or transaction, adopted by **Theodore Roosevelt** for his guiding principle of governance. As he explained at the New York State Fair in Syracuse on September 7, 1903, "Let the watchwords of all our people be the old familiar watchwords of honesty, decency, fair-dealing, and commonsense . . . We must treat each man on his worth and merits as a man. We must see that each is given a square deal, because he is entitled to no more and should receive no less. The welfare of each of us is dependent fundamentally upon the welfare of all of us."

Roosevelt's promise of "A Square Deal for Every Man" got top billing as an election slogan, but there were also "The Big Stick," "Win with Teddy," "Stand Pat," "Theodore Roosevelt, One and Indivisible," and "Same Old Flag and Victory."

SQUATTER. Someone who settles on land or property to which he or she has no legal title. This word was first recorded by **James Madison** in a letter to George Washington in 1788, while the Constitution, which had been adopted by the Constitutional Convention, had yet to be ratified. In a discussion of his and Washington's "hopes and fears," he wrote, "Many of them [representatives of the Province of Maine] and their constituents are only squatters upon other people's land, and they are afraid of being brought to account."[140]

STATE OF THE UNION. The annual address presented by the president of the United States to a joint session of Congress. The speech was referred to as "the President's Annual Message to Congress" until 1934, when the term "State of the Union" was coined and applied by President **Franklin D. Roosevelt**.

George Washington gave the first annual address to Congress on January 8, 1790. In 1801, Thomas Jefferson discontinued the practice of giving the speech in person, and the address was read by a congressional clerk until 1913, when Woodrow Wilson once again gave a live speech. Calvin Coolidge's 1923 address was the first broadcast on radio, Harry Truman's 1947 speech was the first broadcast on television, and Bill Clinton's 1997 address was the first broadcast available live on the Internet.[141]

STRATEGERY. (1) a vague secret plan behind an act of maneuvering; (2) the improvisational work of political consultant. This word was actually coined in 2000 by the comedian Will Ferrell on *Saturday Night Live* to mock **George W. Bush**'s oratory skills. Bush never used the word in public, but it became a running joke in the White House afterward. Nonetheless, Bush is still given credit for what amounts to a faux Bushism.[142]

TEDDY BEAR. A stuffed toy bear of plush or similar material, so-called after **Theodore "Teddy" Roosevelt**, a noted big-game hunter. In 1902, he took a few days off to go bear hunting in Mississippi. The hunt was a failure, because the president was unable to find a bear to kill. On the last day of the hunt, one of his friends brought a bear cub into camp as a joke and told the great hunter he might shoot it. Roosevelt took one look at the sad little creature and, according to the most commonly repeated versions of the story, said, "Take it away. I draw the line. If I shot that little fellow, I couldn't look my own boys in the face again."

When the president got back to Washington, he told his good friend Clifford K. Berryman, a cartoonist at the *Washington Post*, about the incident. Berryman was so amused that he drew a cartoon of it showing Mr. Roosevelt refusing to shoot the bear cub. The bear inspired a German toy company to start manufacturing a line of teddy bears, which were an immediate and continuing hit.

The extension of the term to mean a "big lovable person"

got a boost in 1957, in a song popularized by Elvis Presley, which opened with the line, "Baby, let me be your lovin' teddy bear."

Despite the nickname "Teddy" used for the bear, no member of his family would have dared address Roosevelt by this name.

TEFLON PRESIDENT. Like so many other presidents, **Ronald Reagan** attracted nicknames from the other side of the political aisle, with the most commonly recalled being the *Teflon president* (or Teflon-coated president), because no allegation ever stuck to him, whether it was swapping arms for hostages or influence peddling by cabinet members.

The term was coined by Representative Pat Schroeder (D-CO): "One morning I was scrambling eggs in a Teflon pan for my kids and it suddenly occurred to me: That's what's wrong—this man is the Teflon president: Nothing he does sticks to him ... Although I never heard from Reagan or his team about it, I did get a letter from the lawyers at DuPont, the manufacturer of Teflon, threatening to sue me for trademark infringement. But the real surprise was the response of other politicians ... They mostly asked: How do we get the same protection?"[143]

THOUSAND POINTS OF LIGHT. In his 1989 inaugural address, **George H. W. Bush** invoked the vision of a "thousand points of light" and invited the nation to take action through service to their fellow citizens. He used the metaphor on a number of occasions, including one in which he said, "I have spoken of a thousand points of light—of all the community organizations that are spread like stars throughout the nation, doing good. The old ideas are new again because they are not old, they are timeless: duty, sacrifice, commitment, and a patriotism that finds its expression in taking part and pitching in. This is America . . . a brilliant diversity spread like stars. Like a thousand points of light in a broad and peaceful sky."

The origin of the phrase rests with the speechwriter Peggy Noonan, who may or may not have gotten her inspiration from a poem by W. H. Auden that speaks of "ironic points of light" or a poem by C. S. Lewis published in 1955 that contained the words "a thousand, thousand points of light leaped out." Noonan also gets credit for Bush's pledge, "Read my lips: no new taxes," during his 1988 Republican nomination acceptance speech. (Bush's subsequent reversal of this pledge is often cited as a reason for his loss to Bill Clinton in 1992.)

THREE-MARTINI LUNCH. During his keynote speech at the Democratic National Convention on July 11, 1972, Florida governor **Reuben Askew** vividly illustrated how the system was stacked against the average man and woman: "The business lunch of steak and martinis is tax-deductible, but the workingman's lunch of salami and cheese is not." This symbol of tax inequity was picked up and refined by **George McGovern**, the party's 1972 presidential nominee: "The rich businessman can deduct his three-martini lunch, but you can't take off the price of a baloney sandwich." And later, **Jimmy Carter** termed the three-martini expense-account lunch a disgrace.[144]

THROW ONE'S HAT IN THE RING. **Theodore Roosevelt** popularized the phrase in response to a reporter's question on his way to the Ohio Constitutional Convention in Cleveland in February 1912. Asked whether he intended to run again and confront William Howard Taft (then the current president), the former president replied, "My hat is in the ring; the fight is on and I'm stripped to the buff."

The hat allusion puzzled many, and the *St. Louis Post-Dispatch* asked leading political figures if they understood what Roosevelt meant. There was in fact some confusion. Former Speaker of the House Joe Cannon was one of the confused. "I am a Quaker by birth," he said, "and I always believe in answering questions 'yea, yea' or 'nay, nay.'" The Socialist Victor Berger responded, "Roosevelt has been talking through his hat for so long that in order to finish the job he has cast it into the ring."[145]

Since that time, the phrase "throwing one's hat into the ring" has been associated with entering a political campaign or announcing one's candidacy for office.*

TIN CAN. A vessel made of tinned iron. **George Washington** was the first to enter this Americanism in his diary, in 1770, referring to two Delaware Indians he had hired to carry his canoe: "I was to pay 6 Dollars & give them a Quart Tinn Can."[146]

"TIPPECANOE AND TYLER TOO!" In 1840, **William Henry Harrison** ran on his war record as the hero of the 1811 Battle of Tippecanoe, in which U.S. forces led by Governor Harrison of the Indiana Territory vanquished Native Americans under Tecumseh at the Tippecanoe River. For this, Har-

---

*The ring that year was full of hats. The Democrat, Woodrow Wilson, easily prevailed against TR (Progressive), Taft (Republican), and Eugene V. Debs (Socialist).

rison earned the nickname "Old Tippecanoe." Harrison and his running mate, **John Tyler**, debuted what proved to be the nation's earliest catchy campaign slogan. Harrison won but died a month later, and Tyler became president.

TR. Initialism by which Theodore Roosevelt was known in news headlines; he was the first president to be known popularly by his initials—FDR, HST, DDE, LBJ, and JFK (Franklin Roosevelt, Truman, Eisenhower, Johnson, and Kennedy) followed the trend. Theodore Roosevelt seems to have attracted more nicknames than any other president: "The Great White Chief," "The Happy Warrior," "Haroun-al-Roosevelt," "The Man on Horseback," "The Old Lion," "Telescope Teddy," "Theodore the Meddler," "Wielder of the Big Stick," "The Trust-Buster," "The Typical American," "Old Rough and Ready," "The Hero of San Juan Hill," "The Rough Rider," "The Bull Moose," "The Driving Force," "The Dynamo of Power," and "Four Eyes."

TROCAR. An old word that **Harry Truman** adopted and applied to a new use in politics. A trocar (from the French *trocquart, trois-quart* [1694], *trocart* [1762], *trois* three + *carre* side) is a medical instrument used to channel a fluid from a body cavity. In the context of rural Missouri where Truman was from, a trocar was an instrument (often homemade) that you used to stick into a bull or a cow to relieve bloat. Truman wrote a note (as reported in the *New York Times*) to Michael V. DiSalle, who served as price stabilizer at the Office of Defense Mobilization, after he read DiSalle's criticism of the overinflated egos of Washington fat cats: "Dear Mike, Since I've been in Washington I've seen many stuffed shirts, and your wise-crack about Washington life reminds me of how we used to use a trocar on a clovered [swollen from eating too much clover] bull. There is a loud explosion and the bull resumes his normal shape and usually recovers. Keep sticking 'em."[147]

TRUMAN DOCTRINE. Principle first enunciated by **Harry Truman** in March 1947 that the United States should "support free peoples who are resisting attempted subjugation." Its aim was to keep Europe free of socialism.

TWISTIFICATION. A nonce word created by **Thomas Jefferson** to disparage the decisions of the Supreme Court and its Chief Justice, John Marshall, whose interpretation of the Constitution was not at all to Jefferson's liking. Jefferson alluded frequently to Marshall's "twistifications," and accused him of "rancorous hatred" of the government of his country. He said, "The Supreme Court of the United States can be compared to a subtle corps of sappers and miners, constantly working underground to undermine the foundation of our government, and the independent rights of the state."[148]

UNITED NATIONS. When the first European settlers came to this country, the Iroquois had a union of five tribes. In 1722, the Tuscarora joined the confederation—the Mowhawks, Oneidas, Onondagas, Cayugas, and Senecas. The European settlers usually referred to the Indians of this organization as the Five Nations or the Six Nations, but sometimes they called them the United Nations. Over the years this term passed out of use and was virtually forgotten.

In December 1941, after the Japanese attack on Pearl Harbor, twenty-six nations around the world agreed to cooperate in the great war that was now becoming global. They needed a name for their organization. According to Mitford M. Mathews in *American Words*, "For a time they searched in vain for a suitable title. President **Franklin D. Roosevelt** and Prime Minister Winston Churchill stayed up late on December 30, but could not think of a suitable term.

"The next morning," according to Mathews in one of the more detailed accounts of the incident, "President Roosevelt waked earlier than usual, and as he lay in bed he ran over in his mind suggestions that had been made about a name. As he did so, the expression *United Nations* popped into his mind. He was well pleased with it. He rose at once to go to Mr. Churchill who was his guest at the White House."

The story, as recounted by Roosevelt's adviser Harry Hopkins, was that the prime minister was just emerging from a steaming bathtub, stark naked and flush pink. FDR immediately apologized and promised to come back at a more convenient time. Unflappable as ever, Churchill insisted that there was no need for Roosevelt to leave. He said, "Think nothing of it. The Prime Minister of Great Britain has nothing to conceal from the President of the United States!"*

It was then that Roosevelt asked, "How about the United Nations?" and Churchill assented.

Hopkins recounted the story so many times that it quickly made the rounds in Washington and appeared in print, often embellished with added detail. The Canadian prime minister Mackenzie King duly recorded it in his diary. But was the story as recorded by Mathews and King exactly true? Quoting from the book *One Christmas in Washington: The Secret Meeting between Roosevelt and Churchill That Changed the World*: "When Robert Sherwood, the president's speechwriter, asked Churchill if the story was factual, the prime minister dismissed it as pure 'nonsense.' He never received the president, Churchill informed Sherwood, without at least a bath towel wrapped around him." But the story was too good to go away.

According to *Safire's Political Dictionary*, Churchill later re-

---

*In *American Words*, Mathews tells the story with Churchill still in the tub: "Churchill took a final dip, rinsed the soap from his eyes, and with his face dripping, looked up at his host and said 'That should do it.'"

cited a passage from Lord Byron's 1812 work *Childe Harold's Pilgrimage* to support FDR's choice:

> *Thou fatal Waterloo.*
> *Millions of tongues record thee, and anew*
> *Their children's lips shall echo them and say—*
> *"Here, where the sword united nations drew,*
> *Our countrymen were warring on that day!"*
> *And this is much, and all which will not pass away.*

The name was adopted three years later for the formal international organization.[149]

VANBURENISH. Negative eponym created for **Martin Van Buren**. Van Buren's critics made much of his noncommittalism. "The word *vanburenish*, in fact, was coined to mean evasiveness in politics," wrote Paul F. Boller in *Presidential Campaigns.*[150]

VEEP. The vice president. The Kentuckian **Alben W. Barkley**, who served as vice president from 1949 to 1953, was popularly known by this title. This short item from *Time*, May 23, 1949, titled "The Veep," is definitive: "How do you correctly address the Vice President of the U.S., a reporter wanted to know. Well, said Alben Barkley in a relaxed moment last week, at work some called him Mr. President (because he is president of the Senate). Some called him Mr. Vice President, which is correct according to Emily Post, but a mouthful, and some still call him Senator. 'But my children call me "Veep,"' he confided.

"At week's end, Barkley discovered that he had added a new word to the language. 'Darned if it hasn't gone all over the country now,' he said. 'Every time I pick up a paper I find I'm

'The Veep.'" By the summer, every newspaper in the country was referring to Barkley as "The Veep." When he mentioned that he was contemplating remarriage, the *San Francisco News* carried this headline: "The veep makes an important decision." It was also quickly transferred to others who might be interested in the number-two job: Walter Winchell's column for September 9, 1949, was titled, "Sen. Margaret Smith to Bid for 'Veep'?"

Barkley's successor as vice president, Richard Nixon, declined to continue the nickname, saying that it had been bestowed on Barkley affectionately and belonged to him. While commentators may occasionally use *veep* as a generic word for vice presidents, historically the word is Barkley's alone, but the contest leading up to the selection of a candidate for the office is still referred to as the veepstakes. Today the word is often used in the business world to describe the vice president of a corporation.[151]

Barkley, who was the last important American politician born in a log cabin, was noted as the master of the illustrative anecdote. One of the most famous was dubbed "Barkley's True Story of the Ungrateful Constituent."

"He's a farmer down home," Barkley recalled. "During the First World War, I got his allotment fixed and his Government insurance. Then he was wounded in Belleau Wood—and I went to see him in the hospital over in France. After the Armistice, I wrote a personal letter to get him back home. I got him a loan for his farm. A couple years later a big flood nearly washed his farm away—so I got him a Disaster Loan and a job for his wife as a postmistress.

"In 1938 when Happy Chandler ran against me for the

Senate nomination I heard this farmer was 'agin' me. I went around to see him and asked him: 'Is it true that you're not going to vote for me?' He just nodded."

Choking with rage, Barkley ticked off all the favors he'd performed for his constituent, ending, "Surely you must remember all those things I've done for you?"

"Yeah," admitted the farmer grudgingly, "but what the hell have you done for me *lately*?"[152]

VOODOO ECONOMICS. Pejorative term for supply-side tax theory, coined by **George H. W. Bush** in his 1980 campaign for the Republican nomination. Bush used the term to describe Ronald Reagan's promise to cut taxes, boost defense spending, and balance the budget by 1983.

VOTE EARLY AND VOTE OFTEN. This phrase first appeared in 1848, when it was attributed to John Van Buren, son of Free Soil candidate **Martin Van Buren**. Although this attribution comes from secondary sources, the phrase was in full play by the middle of the nineteenth century. An editorial in the *New York Times* of September 24, 1858, talked of a class of voters who were "dissipated, reckless and venal," and who "vote early and vote often." A year later the *Hartford Courant* (June 24, 1859) reported that "fifty patriotic democrats, who obeyed the party instructions to 'vote early and vote often' at the recent Kansas elections, are now in jail in Leavenworth for the fraud."

WALL OF SEPARATION BETWEEN CHURCH AND STATE. Coined by President **Thomas Jefferson** in a carefully crafted letter to the Danbury Baptists in 1802, when they asked him to explain the First Amendment. The Supreme Court and lower courts have used Jefferson's phrase repeatedly in major decisions upholding neutrality in matters of religion. The exact words "separation of church and state" do not appear in the Constitution; neither do "separation of powers," "interstate commerce," "right to privacy," and other phrases describing well-established constitutional principles.

WAR ON DRUGS. A term coined by **Richard Nixon** in 1972.

WAR ON TERROR. In the wake of the attacks of September 11, 2001, this term was coined by **George W. Bush** and first used in his September 20, 2001, speech to Congress.*

---

*The term "weapons of mass destruction," which came into play in the days after 9/11 and during the ramp up to the Iraqi War, did not originate with the Bush administration but rather was coined by Cosmo Gordon Lang, archbishop of

WAR ROOM. A room where maps showing the current status of troops in battle are maintained. By extension, any room used for conferences and planning, which is often specially equipped for the purposes of running a campaign (telephones, charts, computers etc.). **William McKinley** was the first president to make extensive use of the telephone, which he used along with the telegraph to keep in contact with the military headquarters in the field as well as commands in the field during the Spanish-American War, the first war to be managed from a White House command center. Kevin Phillips made this point in his McKinley biography. A "war room," outfitted with maps, markers, and communications equipment, was set aside as war with Spain became imminent. The term was used by the McKinley administration and quickly showed up in newspapers. It first appeared in the *Boston Globe* on May 2, 1898, after the U.S. Fleet had beaten the Spanish at Manila Bay, under the banner headline: HAVANA NEXT: "In the 'war room' of the white house McKinley sat by the telegraph instrument receiving the bulletins as they came hurrying in over the wire." On July 6, 1898, an item in the *Zion's Herald* discussed the stress under which McKinley was working: "It is four months since he has taken any respite from

Canterbury, in 1937, referring to aerial bombing campaigns of the Spanish Civil War of that year, and in particular the Nazi bombing attack on the Spanish city of Guernica.

White House duties. He will not even go out to the Soldiers' Home Park where Lincoln and other Presidents occupied during the hot months, but will remain in the White House and be near the 'war room.'"

It was later asserted that McKinley was the first president to actually take charge of the nation's ground and naval forces as commander in chief directing operations from the White House. The incident that drove home this point involved General William "Pecos Bill" Shafter on the ground in Cuba, who telegraphed McKinley that he and his troops were cornered and faced having to surrender to the Spanish. Shafter was told by return telegram that U.S. ships were entering Santiago Harbor, reinforcements were on their way, and he should hold his ground.[153]

WAR TO END ALL WARS. A phrase used optimistically to describe World War I, commonly ascribed to **Woodrow Wilson** but in fact coined by **H. G. Wells** in 1914 in a slightly different form as the title of his book *The War That Will End War*. In 1934, Wells claimed the descriptor as his own in an article in *Liberty* magazine. A cynical version of the quote has been attributed to David Lloyd George, British prime minister during the second half of the war, who said, "This war, like the next war, is a war to end war."[154]

WASHINGTON. The U.S. capital, founded in 1791, was named for **George Washington**, as was the state in the far Northwest when it was formed as a territory in 1853 (admitted to the union 1889). George Washington was probably named after George Eskridge, a lawyer in whose charge his mother had been left when she was orphaned. The family name came from a town in northeastern England, from Old English, literally "estate of a man named Wassa."

WASHINGTONIAN. A believer in the Federalist principles of George Washington. A resident of Washington, D.C.

WATCHFUL WAITING. Term coined by **Woodrow Wilson** to refer to America's relations with Mexico during its revolutionary period under the dictatorship of Victoriano Huerta. In his annual message to Congress on December 2, 1913, Wilson said of the situation, "We shall not, I believe, be obliged to alter our policy of watchful waiting [to decide whether to recognize Huerta as president]."

By extension, the term was used to refer to the policy of neutrality toward Europe during Wilson's first administration. Others adapted it to their own use. A June 16, 1918, headline in the *Detroit Free Press*—"'Watchful Waiting' Policy Adopted by Generals of Baseball These Days"—alluded to uncertainty about the fate of baseball during the war.

In recent times, "watchful waiting" describes doctors allowing time to pass before initiating medical intervention or therapy.

WEASEL WORDS. A label for heavily qualified speech, coined by **Theodore Roosevelt** (who originally used the term *weasel phrases*), to describe "a typical vice of American politics—the avoidance of saying anything real on real issues, and the announcement of radical policies with much sound and fury, and at the same time with a cautious accompaniment of weasel phrases each of which sucks the meat out of the preceding statement."

WEE-WEED UP. A coarse neologism created by President **Barack Obama** in the summer of 2009 to describe Washington, D.C.'s agitated state of mind: "There's something about August going into September where everybody in Washington gets all wee-weed up. I don't know what it is. But that's what happens."

Sarah Palin agreed that that's what happens. In 2012, when Rick Santorum was running for the Republican presidential nomination, he gave a speech that included the statement, "Satan has his sights on the United States of America." According to Palin, "The lamestream media [got] all wee-weed up about that."

"WHAT THIS COUNTRY NEEDS IS A GOOD FIVE-CENT CIGAR." Coinage of Woodrow Wilson's vice president, **Thomas Marshall**, whose lasting contribution to American history is this line, which at one time was so oft quoted that any sentence that started with the words "What this country needs is . . ." was called a Marshallism. The original comment from Marshall attracted all sorts of mock-laudatory comment. An editorial in the *Baltimore Sun* called it "a wise, sagacious, profound and truly philosophic remark" and described Marshall as "that homely and homespun Hoosier."[155]

WHISTLE-STOP CAMPAIGN/WHISTLE-STOP TOUR. *Whistle stop* was established slang for a small railroad station or town at which trains do not stop unless requested by a signal given by a whistle or flag. *Whistle stop* evolved into a term for any small town before Harry Truman's time. In September 1948, when **Harry Truman** was running for reelection, he said that before this campaign was over, he expected to visit every "whistle stop in the United States."

Although Truman gets credit for the construction, he was given a major assist from Senator Robert A. Taft, a man called "Mr. Republican," who gave a speech at the Union League Club in Philadelphia on October 8, 1948, deriding the spectacle of the president of the United States "black-guarding Congress at whistle-stops all across the country." Truman later said that Taft had "invented" the term and given him a leg up. "The Republicans were trying to make fun of my efforts to take the issues in that campaign directly to the people all over the country."

From this came *whistle-stop campaign* and *whistle-stop tour*, describing a political odyssey with many brief stops, and then the use of *whistle-stop* as a verb. For example, "In Michigan last week, nearly 100,000 people turned out to see Eisenhower as he whistle stopped across the state."

Truman's original six tours covered 31,700 miles and took all or part of 44 days, during which he made 356 speeches, averaging 10 per day. It was estimated by *U.S. News & World Report* that the cost per mile was $2.50 (railroad fares, meals, and other living expenses).[156]

WHITE HOUSE SPOKESMAN. Someone who speaks for the president but originally a cover for the president himself. **Warren G. Harding** coined the term, telling reporters to attribute statements he read to them to the spokesman rather than to Harding. His vice president, Calvin Coolidge, took over the practice when he became president, comments Bruce L. Felknor in *Political Mischief: Smear, Sabotage, and Reform in U.S. Elections*: "This practice of not quoting the president directly became the norm for a generation."[157]

WIND DOWN. A term that came into use in connection with the Vietnam War, with evidence to suggest that it was coined by **Richard Nixon** or one of his staff. Used to describe the running down of a clock or the gradual weakening of something formerly strong.

WINDOW OF VULNERABILITY. **Ronald Reagan** coined this phrase to refer to the moment in time when he felt the Soviet Union would be able to wipe out U.S. nuclear weapons capabilities in a single preemptive first strike attack.

WOMEN OF COVER. Term for Muslim women coined by **George W. Bush**, a reference to their religiously prescribed head and body cover. It is a parallel construction to "women of color." The term debuted on October 4, 2001, when Bush said, "I see an opportunity at home when I hear the stories of Christian and Jewish women alike helping women of cover, Arab-American women, go shop because they're afraid to leave their home." Bush used it on a number of occasions in the following weeks and months (October 11, twice on December 4, and twice on January 5, 2002). On December 4, he actually used it to address Muslim women who had come to hear him speak. "I see women of cover here, and I want to thank you for coming from the Muslim community here in America."

XYZ AFFAIR. A diplomatic episode that Americans interpreted as an insult from France. The period from 1798 to 1800 was a time of tension and of maritime brushes between the United States and France. In 1797, President **John Adams** sent Charles Pinckney, John Marshall, and Elbridge Gerry to France to work out an agreement on contested maritime rights. The delegates reported to Washington that they had been approached upon their arrival by three French agents, who demanded a $250,000 bribe to Talleyrand, the French foreign minister, and a loan to France of $10 million before negotiation could begin. The delegates sent home their correspondence with these agents. When Congress demanded to see the documents, Adams gave them copies with the names of the Frenchmen coded X, Y, and Z. The French government denied the authenticity of the correspondence, took offense at its publication, and got its hair up, though only briefly.

In 1939, Wilfred J. Funk, lexicographer and publisher, described a study he had done on presidents as coiners of words and found that Franklin D. Roosevelt had already become the foremost popularizer of phrases among all American presidents. "With most of his second term ahead of him," Dr. Funk said in an interview with the Associated Press, "the President should set a mark difficult for any successor to surpass. He and his aides have been unprecedentedly adept in crystallizing phrases that are quickly comprehensible, attach themselves to the memory easily and fit into headlines readily." He listed *New Deal*, *the forgotten man*, *modern Tories*, *economic Royalists*, *princes of privilege*, *gold hoarders*, *democratize industry*, *off the record*, *fireside chat*, *the more abundant life*, *pump priming*, *brain trust*, *quarantine of nations*, *planned economy*, *Good Neighbor Policy*, and the general alphabetizing of the functions of government. In his analysis, the dictionary publisher added that "an out-cropping of phrases traceable to the New Deal includes such expressions as 'The 59 Cent Dollar,' 'Soak the Rich,' 'Boondoggling,' 'Alphabet Soup,' and 'Packing the Court.'"

But Franklin Roosevelt must still take a backseat to Theodore Roosevelt, Dr. Funk said, in the coining or popularizing of expressions that "attract the attention of dictionary makers." Among them he listed *trust-busting, mollycoddle, square deal, frazzle, nature-faking, bull moose, pussy-footing,* and *weasel words.*

"The former President Roosevelt invented a word as well as a phrase in his warning not to 'chinafy' America while he was pleading for preparedness," said Dr. Funk. "Among his other famous expressions were 'the strenuous life,' 'speak softly but carry a big stick,' 'predatory wealth,' 'undesirable citizens,' 'my spear knows no Brother,' and 'we stand at Armageddon and battle for the Lord.'"

Funk's analysis notwithstanding, using the *Oxford English Dictionary* and its "first evidence for word" credits Thomas Jefferson with 110 new words and 382 new senses for older words, with an overall 1,850 quotations in the dictionary. Jefferson is ranked at 214 among the *OED*'s 1,000 top sources, between George Meredith and Nathaniel Hawthorne. Second to Jefferson of American presidents is George Washington, who ranks 916 in the *OED*, with 32 examples for the first evidence for a word. In his book *Presidential Voices*, Allan Metcalf addressed this very question in a chapter titled "Presidents as Neologists" before deciding on the top man and the top ten words invented or promoted by presidents, listed in presidential order:

administration (Washington)

caucus (John Adams)

lengthy (Adams), lengthily (Jefferson)

belittle (Jefferson)

muckraker (Theodore Roosevelt)

lunatic fringe (TR)

bloviation (Harding)

normalcy (Harding)

misunderestimate (George W. Bush)

embetterment (GWB)

Metcalf then concluded that Jefferson and George W. Bush ("Tom" and "Dubya," as he referred to them) top the list of neologists: "Tom because he advocated neology—the coining of new words—as well as practiced it; Dubya because—well, it's hard to misunderestimate his contributions to the English language."[2]

My own appraisal of the top man is Theodore Roosevelt, including both words and phrases. In this case, it is not the volume but the quality and sharpness of his constructions.

ACKNOWLEDGMENTS

At the Library of Congress: Gary Johnson in the Periodicals Reading Room and, as ever, Tom Mann, the Emperor of Reference Librarians, helped me through many of the knottiest problems faced in this book.

Carol Grant of the Tacoma, Washington, Public Library, helped me track down citations in the stacks of that absolute gem of a public library where I had the pleasure of having a few days to work.

Last but not least, my deepest thanks to Bill Young and Nancy Dickson, whose editorial assistance was invaluable.

NOTES

I. INTRODUCTION: BRAVE NEW WORDS

1. Baugh and Cable, *A History of the English Language*, p. 355.
2. Mathews, *American Words*, p. 73.
3. Mencken, *The American Language*, p. 28.
4. Word Study 27, no. 4 (April 1952): 4, quoting from an article in the *Springfield Republican*, July 8, 1865.
5. Evans, "Presidents Vs. The King's English, p. 2; *Word Study*, May 1946, p. 3.
6. Evans, "Presidents Vs. The King's English."
7. Mark Liberman, "You Say Nevada, I Say Nevahda," Language Log, January 3, 2004.

II. HAIL TO THE WHITE HOUSE

1. Ciardi, *A Browser's Dictionary*, pp. 5–6.
2. *The Papers of Woodrow Wilson* (Princeton: Princeton University Press, 1980), 3:38.
3. *The Writings of Thomas Jefferson*, ed. Andrew Adgate Lipscomb and Albert Ellery Bergh, 20 vols. (Washington, D.C.: Thomas Jefferson Memorial Association, 1904), 9:409; Theodore Roosevelt, letter to S. Stanwood Menken of the Congress of Constructive Patriotism, January 10, 1917. Roosevelt's sister Corinne, Mrs. Douglas Robinson, read the letter to a national meeting, January 26, 1917. *Proceedings of the Congress of Constructive Patriotism* (Washington, D.C.: National Security League, January 25–27, 1917), p. 172.

4. Craigie and Hulbert, *Dictionary of American English*, 1:25; *The Correspondence and Public Papers of John Jay*, 4 vols. (New York: Putnam, 1890–9), 4:242.
5. *Oxford English Dictionary*, 1698 R. BOULTON *Exam. Mr. J. Colbatch Bks.* 138 "I shall here confute what he hath said, by his own Words, we are therefore to believe, that all Bodies, from which can be drawn by Chymical Analization, a Volatile Oyl, are Acids." There are many other examples given, up to and including: 1994 *Calgary* (Alberta) *Herald* (Nexis) 10 Sept. E1 "The structure . . . was built without nails, and the wood—after professional analyzation—does not come from anywhere on this continent."
6. Craigie and Hulbert, *Dictionary of American English*, Vol. I., p. 51; www.monticello.org/site/research-and-collections/review-andrew-burstein.
7. The *Oxford English Dictionary*'s first two citations for this word are both from Adams. 1782 J. ADAMS *Let.* in P. Smith *John Adams* (1962) 1.511 "It will be a fright and terror to the Anglomanes."
8. Craigie and Hulbert, *Dictionary of American English*, 1:51; *The Writings of Thomas Jefferson*, 6:125.
9. Metcalf and Barnhart, *America in So Many Words*, p. 96.
10. *The Writings of Thomas Jefferson*, 7:238.
11. *The Papers of George Washington: Retirement Series*, ed. W. W. Abbott (Charlottesville: University Press of Virginia, 1998), 1:314.
12. Bush, *Decision Points*, p. 233.
13. Robert Hendrickson, *The Facts on File Encyclopedia of Word and Phrase Origins* (New York: Facts on File, 1987); Tom Meany, *Babe Ruth: The Big Moments of the Big Fellow* (New York: A. S. Barnes, 1947).
14. *Oxford English Dictionary*, 1786 G. WASHINGTON *Diary* 9 May (1925) III. 58.
15. *Public Papers of the Presidents of the United States: John F. Kennedy, 1961* (Washington, D.C.: Government Printing Office, 1964), pp. 404–05.
16. Eleanor Berman, *Thomas Jefferson Among the Arts: An Essay in Early American Esthetics* (New York: Philosophical Library, 1947), p. 223; Mencken, *The American Language, Supplement One*, p. 36; Read, *Milestones in the History of English in America*, p. 50 (the quote from the *European Magazine* is in the issue of August, 1787, 114n); Fitzedward Hall, *Recent Exemplifications of False Philology* (New York: Scribner, Armstrong, 1872), p. 102; Pyles, *Words and Ways of American English*, p. 18.
17. Metcalf, *Presidential Voices*, p. 130.
18. http://articles.baltimoresun.com/2011-10-10/news/bs-md-in-a-

word-1010-20111010_1_bloviate-evocative-word-word-blow; *Oxford English Dictionary*, 1845 *Huron Reflector* (Norwalk, Ohio), 14 Oct. 3/1; Frank Rich, "The Bloviators' Ball," *New York Times*, January 6, 1999, p. A-23; Metcalf, *Presidential Voices*, p. 135.

19. *Washington Post*, April 21, 1934. p. 1.
20. Metcalf, *Presidential Voices*, p. 132.
21. Metcalf and Barnhart, *America in So Many Words*, p. 253; Safire, *Safire's Political Dictionary*, pp. 83–84.
22. Mathews, *Dictionary of Americanisms*, 1:198–99.
23. www.theodoreroosevelt.org/research/speech kill moose.htm.
24. "The Roosevelt Administration," *New York Times*, March 4, 1909, p. 8; *Springfield Daily Republican*, August 2, 1909, p. 6.
25. Metcalf and Barnhart, *America in So Many Words*, p. 70.
26. Flexner, *Listening to America*, p. 142.
27. Dohan, *Our Own Words*; *Oxford English Dictionary*, 1908 H. G. WELLS *New Worlds for Old* xiii. 305.
28. *The Oxford English Dictionary*, 1787 T. JEFFERSON *Corr.* (1829) II. 162.
29. *The Word Blog*, posted by Jan Freeman, September 21, 2008, Boston. com.
30. Leibovich, "Pedal to the Metal."
31. *New York Times*, December 22, 1946; Safire, *Safire's Political Dictionary*, pp. 156–57.
32. *The Writings of Thomas Jefferson*, 7:445.
33. *Oxford English Dictionary*, 1583 G. PECKHAM *True Rep. Newfound Landes* vii. sig. H.j.
34. Stanley I. Kutler, ed., *Abuse of Power: The New Nixon Tapes* (New York: Free Press, 1997), pp. 149–50.
35. *Papers of Thomas Jefferson*, 12:447; *Writings of George Washington*, 39 vols. (Washington, D.C.: Government Printing Office, 1940), 34:355, 401.
36. Stephen E. Ambrose, "Comparing and Contrasting Ike and Dick," in *Richard M. Nixon: Politician, President, Administrator*, ed. Leon Friedman and William F. Levantrosser (Westport, CT: Greenwood Press, 1991), p. 17.
37. *Washington Post*, October 4, 1949, p. B-3.
38. Curtis D. MacDougall, *Understanding Public Opinion: A Guide for Newspapermen and Newspaper Readers* (New York: Macmillan, 1952), p. 195.
39. Frank Moss, *American Metropolis, from Knickerbocker Days to the Present Time* (New York: Collier, 1897), I. ii. 266 Motto.
40. Dillard, *American Talk*, p. 141.
41. Flexner, *I Hear America Talking*, p. 255.

42. Carl Sferrazza Anthony points out a possible coinage in *First Ladies: The Saga of the Presidents' Wives and Their Power, 1789–1961* (New York: William Morrow, 1990); Craigie and Hulbert, *Dictionary of American English*, Vol. III p. 1825; *Boston Globe*, August 17, 1994; Margaret Truman, *First Ladies: An Intimate Group Portrait of White House Wives* (New York: Random House, 1995), p. 30.

43. Richard Hanser, "Of Deathless Remarks . . . ," *American Heritage*, June 1970, p. 57; Harding, "Address on Washington's Birthday," 1918, Senate Doc. 65–180, p. 3; *Chicago Tribune*, November 3, 1918, p. 7. Harding also used the term in his speech on being officially notified of his nomination for the presidency, Marion, Ohio, July 22, 1920; *New York Times*, September 5, 1987, p. 22, and *New York Times Magazine*, May 8, 1988, p. 14; *Chicago Tribune*, August 13, 1929, p. 6.

44. President Franklin D. Roosevelt, State of the Union message to the Congress, January 6, 1941, *The Public Papers and Addresses of Franklin D. Roosevelt*, 13 vols. (New York: Random House, 1941), 10:672.

45. *Aberdeen American*, September 28, 1910, p. 1; *New York Times*, February 25, 1912.

46. *Los Angeles Times*, October 25, 1900, p. 115.

47. *Oxford English Dictionary*, 1840 J. Q. ADAMS *Jrnl.* 11 Feb. in *Mem.* (1876) X. 216.

48. H. L. Mencken, *A Carnival of Buncombe* (Baltimore: Johns Hopkins University Press, 1956), p. 42.

49. Goulden, "Give 'em Hell, Harry."

50. Congressional Record, vol. 89, p. 761.

51. www.theodoreroosevelt.org/life/Maxwell.htm; www.barrypopik.com/index.php/new_york_city/entry/good_to_the_last_drop/.

52. Webber and Feinsilber, *Grand Allusions*, pp. 148–49.

53. Ciardi, *A Second Browser's Dictionary*, p. 120.

54. *The Writings of George Washington*, ed. Worthington Chauncey Ford, 14 vols. (New York: Putnam, 1889–93), 1:299; Safire, *Safire's Political Dictionary*, p. 309; *Time*, October 23, 1944, p. 20: "Exuberant hatchet jobs were done on Foster Dulles because of his Wall Street connections"; Mathews, *Dictionary of Americanisms*, Vol. I, p. 782.

55. Webber and Feinsilber, *Grand Allusions*, pp. 161–62. The Adams reference is from an 1818 letter to Hezekiah Niles, publisher *of Niles' Weekly Register*.

56. H. B. Gross in the *New York Tribune*, June 13, 1917.

57. *Parade*, May 23, 1954; Safire, *Safire's Political Dictionary*, p. 325.

58. *The Collected Works of Abraham Lincoln*, ed. Roy P. Basler, 8 vols. (New Brunswick, NJ: Rutgers University Press, 1953), 2:461.

59. John Adams and Charles Francis Adams, *The Works of John Adams, Second President of the United States* (Boston: Little, Brown, 1856), p. 86.

60. "Roosevelt Bars the Hyphenated," *New York Times*, October 13, 1915.

61. *New York Times*, January 6, 1933.

62. Harry S. Truman, *Mr. Citizen* (New York: Bernard Geis, 1960), p. 229.

63. John Crosby, "Have the TV Debates Cost Nixon the Election?" *Washington Post*, October 26, 1960, p 36.

64. Ralph E. Weber, *Masked Dispatches: Cryptograms and Cryptology in American History, 1775–1900* (Washington, D.C.: Center for Cryptologic History, National Security Agency, 1993), p. 69.

65. Thomas Jefferson, *The Jeffersonian Cyclopedia: A Comprehensive Collection of the Views of Thomas Jefferson*, ed. John P. Foley (New York: Funk and Wagnalls, 1900), p. 453.

66. *Oxford English Dictionary*, 1799 G. WASHINGTON *Writings* (1893) XIV. 229.

67. *Hartford Courant*, June 11, 1973, p. 26.

68. Theodore Roosevelt, *Theodore Roosevelt: An Autobiography* (New York: Macmillan, 1913), p. 625.

69. *The Writings of George Washington*, 2:163; Metcalf, *Presidential Voices*, p. 11.

70. Dohan, *Our Own Words*, p. 202.

71. Craigie and Hulbert, *A Dictionary of American English*, Vol II. p. 1337.

72. Mencken, *The American Language, Supplement One*, pp. 280; Paul F. Boller Jr., *Presidential Campaigns*, rev. ed. (New York: Oxford University Press, 1996), p. 67.

73. Brands, *Andrew Jackson*, p. 416; Arthur Charles Cole, *The Whig Party in the South* (Washington, D.C.: American Historical Association, 1913), p. 13.

74. *New York Times*, November 5, 1919, p. 2; Donald R. McCoy, *Calvin Coolidge: The Quiet President* (New York: Macmillan, 1967), p. 114.

75. *Bismarck Tribune*, March 6, 1925, p. 4.

76. *Writings of Thomas Jefferson*, 6:391.

77. *Oxford English Dictionary*, J. ADAMS *Diary* 3 Jan. (1961) I. 72; Pyles, *Words and Ways of American English*, p.19.

78. William Allen White, *The Autobiography of William Allen White*, 2nd ed. (Lawrence: University Press of Kansas, 1990), p. 174.

79. Theodore Roosevelt, *History as Literature and Other Essays* (New York: Scribner, 1913), p. 305; Theodore Roosevelt, *An Autobiography* (New York: Scribner, 1922), p. 206.

80. *Forum*, February 1895, Memorial Edition 15, p. 10, National Edition 13, p. 9.

81. *Oxford English Dictionary*, 1801 T. Jefferson *Let.* 22 Oct. in *Papers* (2008) XXXV. 479.

82. Ibid., J. O'Sullivan in *U.S. Mag. & Democratic Rev.* July–Aug. 5.

83. McCullough, *Truman*, p. 669.

84. *The Political Writings of Thomas Jefferson*, ed. Merrill D. Peterson (Monticello, VA: Thomas Jefferson Foundation, 1993), p. 39.

85. Oxford English Dictionary, 1848 A. Lincoln *Coll. Wks.* (1953) I. 509.

86. *Daily Telegraph*, July 21, 2010; Metcalf, *Presidential Voices*, p. 137; "Snow Job," *Washington Times*, December 27, 2010.

87. *Pendennis* (1850) I. xxxii. 310

88. *New York Times*, February 24, 1907; *Washington Post*, March 7, 1907, p. 9; *Chicago Tribune*, April 21, 1908, p. 6; Theodore Roosevelt, "The Panama Canal," in *The Pacific Ocean in History*, ed. H. Morse Stephens and Hebert E. Bolton (New York: Macmillan, 1917), p. 149.

89. Nathan Schachner, *Thomas Jefferson: A Biography* (New York: Thomas Yoseloff, 1957), p. 407; *Oxford English Dictionary*, 1793 T. Jefferson *Let.* 29 June in *Papers* (1995) XXVI. 401; *Baltimore Sun*, October 23, 1954, p. 24.

90. *Oxford English Dictionary*, 1848 I. E. Holmes in *Congress. Globe* 29 Apr. 711; 1850 *Debow's Rev.* 9 176: "The Monroe doctrine, without doubt, has been stretched far beyond its original intention."

91. *Economist*, September 1, 1962, 780/1: "The . . . taunts of 'moondoggle' . . . when Mr Kennedy first outlined his plans for exploring the moon."

92. *Christian Science Monitor*, May 17, 1977, p. 32.

93. *Oxford English Dictionary*, 1788 *Rep. on Commerce* 15 Oct. in T. Jefferson *Papers* (1956) XIII. 67.

94. Maurice Garland Fulton, ed., *Roosevelt's Writings* (New York: Macmillan, 1920), p. 263; "T.R. and the 'Nature Fakers,'" *American Heritage*, February 1971.

95. *Oxford English Dictionary*, 1813 T. Jefferson *Let.* 16 Aug. in *Writings* (1984) 1300; Metcalf, *Presidential Voices*, p. 110.

96. Alter, *The Defining Moment*, p. 117; Samuel Rosenman, *Working with Roosevelt* (New York: Harper, 1952). The full account of the interview and the medal presentation appears in Cyril Clemens, "F. D. Roosevelt and Mark Twain," *Dalhousie Review*, October 1945; the fullest discussion of this term is in Holland, "New Light on 'New Deal.'"

97. *New York Times*, July 16, 1960, p. 1.

98. *Gulf News*, September 1, 2008.

99. www.theatlanticwire.com/politics/2011/10/who-coined-obamacare/44183/; *Washington Post*, July 21, 2012, p. A15.

100. *Writings of George Washington*, 4:385.

101. Ruth Marcus, "In Transition to Twilight Zone, Clinton's Every Word Is Scrutinized," *Washington Post*, November 22, 1992, p. A1; *New Republic*, April 6, 1992, p. 20.

102. The first three citations in the *OED* are from 1839; this is the first: C. G. GREENE in *Boston Morning Post* 23 Mar. 2/2 "He . . . would have the 'contribution box,' et ceteras, *o.k.*—all correct—and cause the corks to fly, like *sparks*, upward."

103. *Works of Thomas Jefferson*, 5:78, letter of February 8, 1786.

104. *Oxford English Dictionary*, 1789 T. JEFFERSON *Memorandum Bks.* 19 Aug. (1997) 1. 740.

105. Dennis Hevesi, "Robert Hartmann, 91, Dies; Wrote Ford's Noted Talk," *New York Times*, April 19, 2008.

106. *The Papers of Thomas Jefferson*, ed. J. Jefferson Looney, 8 vols. (Princeton: Princeton University Press, 2009), 5:409, letter of October 23, 1812.

107. Theodore Roosevelt, *Hunting Trips of a Ranchman: Sketches of Sport on the Northern Cattle Plains* (New York: Putnam, 1885), p. 19.

108. *Oxford English Dictionary*, 1782 G. WASHINGTON *Let.* 13 Oct. in *Writings* (1931) XXV. 256.

109. Ibid., 1784 T. JEFFERSON *Memorandum Bks.* 29 Dec. (1997) I. 571.

110. *New York Times*, March 5, 1998, p. B-5, and March 6, 1998, p. E-44.

111. William Safire, "Nine Little Words," *New York Times*, March 26, 1989.

112. *New York Times*, October 19, 1947.

113. John Spencer Bassett, *Epochs of American History: Expansion and Reform, 1889–1926* (New York: Longmans, Green, 1935), p. 235.

114. Miller, *Plain Speaking*, pp. 131–32.

115. Research conducted by Louis Milliner of New Orleans for the *Dickson Word Treasury*.

116. Bruce L. Felknor, *Political Mischief: Smear, Sabotage, and Reform in U.S. Elections* (Westport, CT: Praeger, 1992), p. 199; www.questia.com/read/28649106; *U.S. News & World Report*, September 4, 1978.

117. Rexford Guy Tugwell, *Grover Cleveland* (New York: Macmillan, 1968), p. 82.

118. *Oxford English Dictionary*, 1911 *Bismarck* (N. Dakota) *Daily Tribune* 19 Apr. 3/2; *OED*, 1916 *Williamsburg* (Iowa) *Jrnl.-Tribune* 13 Apr. 4/3; Marckwardt, *American English*.

119. Adams, *The Works of John Adams*, p. 157; Craigie and Hulbert, *Dictionary of American English*, Vol. III,p. 1877.

120. *A Compilation of the Messages and Papers of the Presidents* (New York: Bureau of National Literature, 1897), 9:3605.

121. *Writings of George Washington*, GPO, 9:13; *Writings of George Washington*, ed. Jared Sparks (Boston: Little, Brown 1858), 11:414.

122. *Oxford English Dictionary*, 1775 G. WASHINGTON *Gen. Orders* 14 July in *Papers* (1985) Revolutionary War Ser. I. 115.

123. Ibid., 1793 G. WASHINGTON *Let.* 10 June in *Papers* (2007) Presidential Ser. XIII. 55.

124. Ted Sorensen, *Counselor: A Life at the Edge of History* (New York: Harper, 2008), p. 140.

125. Felknor, *Political Mischief*, p. 119; "Beware of Baron Roorback," *Chicago Daily Tribune*, October 23, 1940, p. 14.

126. *Century Magazine* 35, no. 4 (February 1888).

127. *Christian Science Monitor*, November 4, 1946; "Name of 'Sacred Cow' for Truman's Plane Causes Embarrassment at White House," *New York Times*, October 27, 1946.

128. *Memoirs, Correspondence, and Private Papers of Thomas Jefferson* (London: Colburn & Bentley, 1829), 1:121.

129. *Oxford English Dictionary*, 1770 T. JEFFERSON *Memorandum Bks.* 27 Dec. (1997); 1788 F. GROSE *Classical Dict. Vulgar Tongue* (ed. 2) "*Shag*, to copulate."

130. *New York Times*, June 13, 1920, p. 5.

131. *Public Papers of the Presidents of the United States: Richard Nixon* (Washington, D.C.: GPO, 1999), p. 909; Shenker, *Harmless Drudges*, p. 14.

132. *Word Study*, October 1932, p. 4, and December 1932, p. 4.

133. *Encyclopedia of Chicago* (Chicago: Newberry Library, 2004); William Safire, "Smoke-Filled Room," in *The New Language of Politics: An Anecdotal Dictionary of Catchwords, Slogans, and Political Usage* (New York: Random House, 1968); Andrew Sinclair, *The Available Man: The Life Behind the Masks of Warren Gamaliel Harding* (New York: Macmillan, 1965).

134. Mencken, *The American Language, Supplement One*, p. 241; *Oxford English Dictionary*, 1940 *Maryland* (Writers' Program) 348.

135. *Oxford English Dictionary*, W. S. CHURCHILL *Let.* 4 Jan. in R. S. Churchill *Winston S. Churchill* (1969) II. Compan. 11. 759.

136. Metcalf and Barnhart, *America in So Many Words*, p. 127. Hawk's recollection of this moment and its context comes twenty-nine years after the event in an interview in the *Boston Herald*, April 11, 1897.

137. *The Works of Theodore Roosevelt*, executive edition, 14 vols. (New York: P. F. Collier, 1901), 13:266, speech, Chicago, April 2, 1903.

138. *The Works of John Adams*, 1:40.

139. John Spencer Bassett, *The Life of Andrew Jackson*, 2 vols. (Garden

City, NY: Doubleday, 1911), 2:447.

140. *Debates on the Adoption of the Federal Constitution*, as reported by James Madison (Philadelphia: Lippincott, 1881), 5:573.

141. PBS, *NewsHour* Extra, "Education and Jobs Are Focus of President Obama's State of the Union Address," January 25, 2011, www.pbs. org/newshour/extra/features/us/jan-june11/sotu_01-25.html.

142. Christopher Borrelli, "English Language Freed!" *Chicago Tribune*, January 20, 2009.

143. Schroeder, *24 Years of House Work*, p. 75.

144. Safire, *Safire's Political Dictionary*, p. 739.

145. *St. Louis Post-Dispatch*, February 23, 1912, p. 9.

146. *Oxford English Dictionary*, 1770 G. WASHINGTON *Diary* 18 Nov. (1925) I. 442.

147. Drew Pearson, "Sunday Morning Truman Note Worries Price Boss DiSalle," *Free Lance-Star*, May 21, 1951, p. 7.

148. William Eleroy Curtis, *The True Thomas Jefferson* (Philadelphia: Lippincott, 1901), p. 79.

149. Bercuson and Herwig, *One Christmas in Washington*, p. 217; Mathews, *American Words*, p. 222; Safire, *Safire's Political Dictionary*, p. 768.

150. Boller, *Presidential Campaigns*, p. 63.

151. *Washington Post*, May 1, 1956, p. 28.

152. *Reader's Digest*, February 1951, pp. 80–81.

153. Phillips, *William McKinley*, p. 81; *Boston Globe*, May 2, 1898, p. 1; *Zion's Herald*, July 6, 1898, p. 76; "How Hartford Men Helped Win '98 War," *Hartford Courant*, June 9, 1922, p. 3 (this article discusses the McKinley war room in some detail).

154. *Boston Globe*, October 1, 1978, p. m-26.

155. *Baltimore Sun*, July 7, 1920, p. 6.

156. Metcalf and Barnhart, *America in So Many Words*, p. 230; Safire, *Safire's Political Dictionary*, pp. 806–07; *Time*, October 13, 1952; *U.S. News & World Report*, October 10, 1952, p. 72.

157. Bruce L. Felknor, *Political Mischief: Smear, Sabotage, and Reform in U.S. Elections* (Westport, CT: Praeger, 1992), p. 199; also *Los Angeles Times*, March 9, 1933, p. 2.

III. THE NEOLOGIST IN CHIEF?

1. *Christian Science Monitor*, February 15, 1938.

2. Metcalf, *Presidential Voices*, p. 110.

BIBLIOGRAPHY

In addition to the works listed below, I used full-text proprietary databases such as 19C (a new database with over a million items from the nineteenth century) and ProQuest Historical Newspapers, which I gained access to through the Library of Congress, the Enoch Pratt Free Library in Baltimore, and the vertical biographical files at the Martin Luther King Jr. Library, Washington, D.C.

Adler, Bill. *Presidential Wit from Washington to Johnson.* New York: Trident Press, 1966.

Alter, Jonathan. *The Defining Moment: FDR's Hundred Days and the Triumph of Hope.* New York: Simon & Schuster, 2006.

Baugh, Albert C., and Thomas Cable. *A History of the English Language.* 5th ed. Englewood Cliffs, NJ: Prentice Hall, 2002.

Bercuson, David J., and Holger H. Herwig. *One Christmas in Washington: The Secret Meeting Between Roosevelt and Churchill That Changed the World.* Woodstock, NY: Overlook, 2005.

Brands, H. W. *Andrew Jackson: His Life and Times.* New York: Doubleday, 2005.

Bryson, Bill. *Made in America: An Informal History of the English Language in the United States.* New York: William Morrow, 1995.

Burrell, Brian. *The Words We Live By: The Creeds, Mottoes, and Pledges That Have Shaped America.* New York: Free Press, 1997.

Bush, George W. *Decision Points.* New York: Crown, 2010.

Calhoun, Harold G. "Slogan Time Is Here Again." *Los Angeles Times,* November 24, 1935, p. 19.

Ciardi, John. *A Browser's Dictionary, and Native's Guide to the Unknown American Language.* New York: Harper, 1980.

————. *A Second Browser's Dictionary, and Native's Guide to the Unknown American Language.* New York: Harper, 1983.

Clay, John E. *Snollygosters, Airheads, and Wimps.* Wilmette, IL: Logolept Press, 1995.

Cole, Donald B. *The Presidency of Andrew Jackson.* Lawrence: University Press of Kansas, 1993.

Craigie, William A., and James R. Hulbert. *A Dictionary of American English on Historical Principles.* 4 vols. Chicago: University of Chicago Press, 1938–44.

Cutten, George B. "WANTED: A SLOGAN TO WIN AN ELECTION: Phrases That Sound Well and Are Sufficiently Indefinite Have Always Been Potent in American Campaigns, and a Clever Catch-Word Will Likely Play an Important Part This Year." *New York Times,* May 13, 1928.

Dean, John W. *Warren G. Harding.* New York: Times Books, 2004.

Dillard, J. L. *American Talk: Where Our Words Came From.* New York: Random House, 1976.

Dohan, Mary Helen. *Our Own Words.* New York: Knopf, 1974.

Donovan, Robert J., ed. *The Words of Harry S. Truman.* New York: Newmarket Press, 1984.

Evans, Bergen. "Presidents Vs. The King's English." *This Week Magazine,* April 13, 1958.

Fields, Wayne. *Union of Words: A History of Presidential Eloquence.* New York: Free Press, 1996.

Flexner, Stuart Berg. *I Hear America Talking: An Illustrated Treasury of American Words and Phrases.* New York: Van Nostrand Reinhold, 1976.

————. *Listening to America: An Illustrated History of Words and Phrases from Our Lively and Splendid Past.* New York: Simon & Schuster, 1982.

Frost, Elizabeth. *The Bully Pulpit: Quotations from America's Presidents.* New York: Facts on File, 1988.

Gardner, Virginia. "The Campaign Slogans of Other Years, the Torchlight Parades for Abraham Lincoln in 1884, Are Recalled by an Exhibit of Presidential Campaign Propaganda." *Chicago Tribune,* September 16, 1936, p. 3.

Gelderman, Carol. *All the Presidents' Words: The Bully Pulpit and the Creation of the Virtual Presidency.* New York: Walker, 1997.

Goulden, Joseph C. "Give 'em Hell, Harry." *Washington Post,* July 25, 1976, p. C-1.

Giffin, Glenn. "Anecdotes of a D.C. Insider: Pat Schroeder's Quips Tap 24 Years in House." *Denver Post*, April 26, 1998, p. E-01.

Harnesberger, Caroline Thomas. *Treasury of Presidential Quotations.* Chicago: Follett, 1964.

Harris, Fred R. *Potomac Fever.* New York: Norton, 1977.

Haskin, Frederic J. *The Presidents and Their Wives.* Washington, D.C.: Haskins Service, 1945.

Holland, Dorothy Garesché. "New Light on 'New Deal.'" *Word Study*, November 1956, pp. 5–8.

Hoover, Herbert. *The Memoirs of Herbert Hoover—The Great Depression, 1929–1941.* New York: Macmillan, 1952.

Jackman, Michael. *Crown's Book of Political Quotations: Over 2500 Lively Quotes from Plato to Reagan.* New York: Crown, 1982.

Jeffers, H. Paul. *An Honest President: The Life and Presidencies of Grover Cleveland.* New York: William Morrow, 2000.

Jones, Taylor. *Add-Verse to Presidents.* New York: Dembner Books, 1982.

Kaltenbach, Chris. "Snappy Slogans." *Baltimore Sun*, November 4, 1984, p. 43.

———. "In the 23 Presidential Elections This Country Has Weathered Thousand Different Campaign Buttons Have Proudly Touted Their Candidates." *Baltimore Sun*, November 4, 1984, p. 43.

Kays, Cecilia. "Roosevelt as a Phrasemaker." *Outlook*, January 7, 1920, pp. 39–40.

Leibovich, Mark. "Pedal to the Metal: The Philosophy That Drives Sen. John McCain." *Washington Post*, May 12, 2004, p. C01.

Library of Congress, comp. *Respectfully Quoted: A Dictionary of Quotations.* Mineola, NY: Dover Publications, 2010.

MacNeil, Robert, and William Cran. *Do You Speak American? A Companion to the PBS Television Series.* New York: Doubleday, 2005.

Mann, Leonard. *A Bird in the Hand: And the Stories Behind 250 Other Common Expressions (The Armchair Philologist).* Englewood Cliffs, NJ: Prentice Hall, 1994.

Marckwardt, Albert H. *American English.* New York: Oxford University Press, 1958.

Mason, Julie. "Bush's First Hurdle Will Be Selling Vision." *Houston Chronicle*, January 16, 2001, p. 1.

Mathews, Mitford M., ed. *Dictionary of Americanisms on Historical Principles.* 2 vols. Chicago: University of Chicago Press, 1951.

———. *American Words.* Cleveland: World Publishing, 1959.

McCormick, Anne O'Hare. "CAMPAIGN SLOGANS EMERGE IN ORATORY: Pattern of Issues, Phrases and Ideas Takes Form in Speeches Before Nominations." *New York Times,* June 29, 1944, p. 15.

McCullough, David. *Truman.* New York: Simon & Schuster, 1992.

McGinnis, Ralph Y., ed. *Quotations from Abraham Lincoln*. Chicago: Nelson-Hall, 1977.

McQuain, Jeffrey. *Never Enough Words: How Americans Invented Expressions as Ingenious, Ornery, and Colorful as Themselves*. New York: Random House, 1999.

Mencken, H. L. *The American Language*. 4th ed. New York: Knopf, 1936 [1919].

———. *The American Language, Supplement One*. New York: Knopf, 1945.

Metcalf, Allan. *Presidential Voices: Speaking Styles from George Washington to George W. Bush*. Boston: Houghton Mifflin, 2004.

Metcalf, Allan, and David K. Barnhart. *America in So Many Words: Words That Have Shaped America*. Boston: Houghton Mifflin, 1997.

Miller, Mark Crispin. *The Bush Dyslexicon: Observations on a National Disorder*. New York: Norton, 2001.

Miller, Merle. *Plain Speaking: An Oral Biography of Harry S. Truman*. New York: Black Dog & Leventhal, 2005.

Morris, Evan. *The Word Detective: Solving the Mysteries Behind Those Pesky Words and Phrases*. Chapel Hill, NC: Algonquin Books, 2000.

Nunberg, Geoffrey. *The Way We Talk Now: Commentaries on Language and Culture from NPR's "Fresh Air."* Boston: Houghton Mifflin, 2001.

Pettey, Tom. "Parties on Hunt for Slogans to Tickle Voters." *Chicago Tribune*, July 15, 1928, p. 16.

Phillips, Kevin. *William McKinley*. New York: Henry Holt, 2003.

Pickering, John. *A Vocabulary; Or, Collection of Words and Phrases Which Have Been Supposed to Be Peculiar to the United States of America*. Cambridge, MA: Hilliard and Metcalf, 1816.

Pyles, Thomas. *Words and Ways of American English*. New York: Random House, 1952.

Rawson, Hugh. "The Words of Watergate." *American Heritage* 48, no. 6 (October 1997): 24.

Read, Allen Walker. *Milestones in the History of English in America*. Durham, NC: Duke University Press, 2002.

Roosevelt, Theodore. *Theodore Roosevelt Cyclopedia*. Rev. 2nd ed. Westport, CT: Meckler Corp., 1989.

Russell, Francis. *Adams: An American Dynasty*. New York: American Heritage, 1976.

Safire, William. "Political Word Watch." *New York Times Magazine*, November 17, 1978.

———. *Safire's Political Dictionary*. 3rd ed. New York: Random House, 1968.

Schroeder, Pat. *24 Years of House Work . . . and the Place Is Still a Mess: My Life in Politics*. Kansas City, MO: Andrews McMeel, 1998.

Shenker, Israel. *Harmless Drudges: Wizards of Language—Ancient, Medieval and Modern*. Bronxville, NY: Barnhart Books, 1979.

Shields-West, Eileen. *The World Almanac of Presidential Campaigns: All the Facts, Anecdotes, and Mudslinging in the History of the Race for the White House.* New York: World Almanac, 1992.

Smith, Mrs. Chetwood. *History's Most Famous Words.* Boston: Lothrop, Lee & Shepard, 1926.

Urdang, Laurence, ed. *Slogans.* 2 vols. Detroit: Gale Research, 1984.

Van Meter, Jan R. *Tippecanoe and Tyler Too: Famous Slogans and Catchphrases in American History.* Chicago: University of Chicago Press, 2008.

Wallraff, Barbara. *Word Fugitives: In Pursuit of Wanted Words.* New York: Harper, 2006.

Ward, John William. *Andrew Jackson: Symbol for an Age.* New York: Oxford University Press, 1962.

Webber, Elizabeth, and Mike Feinsilber. *Grand Allusions: A Lively Guide to Those Expressions, Terms, and References You Ought to Know but Might Not.* Washington, D.C.: Farragut, 1990.

White, Philip. *Our Supreme Task: How Winston Churchill's Iron Curtain Speech Defined the Cold War Alliance.* New York: PublicAffairs, 2012.

AN INDEX OF PROPER NAMES

A NOTE ON THE AUTHOR

PAUL DICKSON has written more than a dozen word books and dictionaries, including *The Dickson Baseball Dictionary*, *The Congress Dictionary* (with Paul Clancy), *Family Words*, and *Slang*. He was a contributing editor with Merriam-Webster in charge of the *Lighter Side of Language* series and did a bylined commentary on language for NPR's *All Things Considered* in the 1990s, and was an occasional contributor to William Safire's "On Language" column in the *New York Times*. Dickson has coined two words of his own: *word word* (the lexical double construction heard in the question, "Are we talking about an e-book or a book book?") and *demonym* (the name for a person from a specific locality, e.g., New Yorker or Hoosier). He is also the author of the seminal narrative history *Sputnik: The Shock of the Century* and the coauthor of the acclaimed *The Bonus Army: An American Epic*. He lives in Garrett Park, Maryland.